HER BREATH BUILT A WORLD

IOANNA MALANDRENIAS

© Copyright Ioanna Malandrenias 2022 - **All rights reserved.**

The content contained within this book may not be reproduced, duplicated or transmitted without direct written permission from the author or the publisher.

Legal Notice:

This book is copyright protected. This book is only for personal use. You cannot amend, distribute, sell, use, quote or paraphrase any part, or the content within this book, without the consent of the author or publisher.

Cover Design by Paper and Sage Designs

Illustrations by Ioanna Malandrenias

ISBN:979-8-9866389-2-8

CONTENTS

INCUBATION	9
FIRST BREATH	14
SING TO ME	50
DANCE WITH ME	81
WE ARE WHAT WE MAKE	127
EMERGENCE	189
FINAL THOUGHTS FROM THE AUTHOR	194
A PRAYER	196
GRATITUDE	197
ABOUT THE AUTHOR	207

*"The Dance-
It Is
The Rhythm
Of
All That Dies
In Order To
Live Again;
It Is
The Eternal Rising
Of
The Sun"*
~Isadora Duncan~

Faith
Beauty
Love
You Are A
Holy Trinity
With Every
Step
In Every
Breath

This Collection
Is Dedicated
To Any Woman
Who Became
The Creatrix
Of
Her Own Life

I Honor You

Her
Breath
Built
A
World

INHALE ~ EXHALE

INCUBATION

Anything we Create is never truly ours. Our Creations are given to us by those Divine Currents that seek a vessel to birth their own desires into this Earthly Realm.

I humbly bow to those forces that chose me as their channel to bring forth these fragrant words. Birthing this work has been one of the most powerful initiations of my life, bringing me into the embrace of the Divine Mother, The Archangels, and of course, those formidable Feminine Frequencies that are coming more and more to the forefront of our spiritual journeys as Women on this planet.

These energies are present in both the Sublime and the Mundane of our daily lives. ESPECIALLY the Mundane. In Pleasure and Pain. Performance. Friendship. Heartbreak. Music. Familial Ties. Erotic Love.

They are the Holy Matrix interwoven with our own fragile mortality, beckoning us to wake up to our inner bridge that links this world to the next. These Infinite Forces are the amniotic fluid that continually births and rebirths us with every breath of this human existence.

A baby Dragonfly found me on the beach today. A Dragonfly incubates underwater until she hatches, becoming a Nymph. She then lives most of her life breathing underwater. One day, her instinct wakes up and guides her to the water's edge, where she prepares for the final shedding of her skin. She then launches into her first Flight. Her Emergence. Like these Nymphs, we spend the beginning our life breathing underwater, preparing to take wing. We must never forget that Emergence and Flight are our Ultimate Destinations. The water's edge awaits...

I humbly bow a second time to you, Dear Reader, for giving your energy to receive this collection. You will notice that throughout the book there are several blank pages with the words "Inhale ~ Exhale" at the top. This is your space to fill with your own thoughts, reactions, activations...exhalations. There is great power in collective inspiration, so let us keep the chain evolving. May these words inspire you like the Divine inspires me each and every day.

The Island of Amorgos
The Cyclades, Greece
November 21st, 2022

INHALE ~ EXHALE

FIRST BREATH

INITIATION

Every Time
You
Exhale
You
Leave
An Opening
For Divinity
To Pass Through
You

Welcome Her

CAGED

When I Can't
Breathe
I Remember
My Lungs
Are
Butterfly Wings
Caged
Within
My Own Flesh

So I Fly

HOLY GROUND

I Walk
On
The Moist Earth
My Feet
Sinking
Into
Holy Ground
The Scent of Winking Lavender Blossoms
Opening
Infiltrates
My Senses
Clings to
My Skin
A Mother's Protection
One Day
I Will Ask
The Oceanids
To Lend
Me
Their Breaths
So I Can
Swim Through
Their Garden of Underwater Wonders

INHALE~EXHALE

A DECISION

Our Bond
Was
Malignant
I
Was
A Fish
With
A Hook
In
Its Mouth
A Decision
To Rip
A Part of Myself
Off
Swim
To Deeper Freedom
Or
Be Pulled Up
On Land
Suffocate
From Too Much Air
I AM
Still Breathing Underwater

LONGING

Your Gaze
Is Where
The Ocean
Meets
The Sunrise
I Long
To Burn
In
Those Azure Waves of Fire

VISION

You Say
That
I'm Beautiful
But
Do You See
My *Beauty?*

MOSAIC

Pieces
Of
My Shattered Spirit
Gleam Like
Abandoned Shards of Sunlight
I Smile
At
My Face
Reflected
In
Their Broken Luminescence
An Iridescent Mosaic
It Is
Now
I Begin
Putting Myself
Back Together
AGAIN

QUIET SPACES

Silence
Is Not
A Lonely Place
It Is
A Life Giving One

MIRROR MIRROR

I Take In
My Battle-Scarred Stare
In The Mirror
And
Whisper
Thank you
I
Feel
Again

WITHIN

I Speak
To Her
My Muse
I Look
For Her
Out There
On
The Glistening Waves
In
The Deepest Earth
Across
The Brightest Skies
Then
I Remember
She Is
In
My Muscles
And
My Marrow

GIFTS

Heaven
Will Give
Me
Wings
When
I Have Given
Myself
Roots

IT'S GREEK TO ME VOL. 1

The Greek Word
For
Inspiration
Means
To Breathe Into
This Holy Inbreathing
All Cyclical
Fully Embodied
We Breathe
Life
Into
Our Creation
Its Spirit
Breathes Back
Into
Us
What
We Make
Makes Us
Eternal

Επηρεύση
Empneusi
Inspiration

MELTING

I AM
Split Open
By
The Stars
That Force
Themselves
Into
Every Crevice
The Moon and Sun
Follow
Heavenly Beings
Conceive Themselves
There
Melting Into
Every Single Vertebra
They Congeal
Into
A Celestial Spinal Fluid
Luminous
Ocean Waves
Release
Over and Over
Again
In My Veins

I AM
Somewhere
In Between
Here and Nowhere
Half Mortal
Half Force
A Wild Centeredness
It Is
Now
When I Truly
Exist

EMBRACE

Things Either
Fall into Place
Or
Fall Apart
Embrace
The Falling
The Universe Knows

Surrender

VOLUME **10**

SUB-HARDY HILBERT SPACES IN THE UNIT DISK

DONALD SARASON
Department of Mathematics
University of California
Berkeley, California

A WILEY-INTERSCIENCE PUBLICATION
JOHN WILEY & SONS, INC.
New York   Chichester   Brisbane   Toronto   Singapore

This text is printed on acid-free paper.

Copyright © 1994 by John Wiley & Sons, Inc.

All rights reserved. Published simultaneously in Canada.

Reproduction or translation of any part of this work beyond that permitted by Section 107 or 108 of the 1976 United States Copyright Act without the permission of the copyright owner is unlawful. Requests for permission or further information should be addressed to the Permissions Department, John Wiley & Sons, Inc., 605 Third Avenue, New York, NY 10158-0012.

Library of Congress Cataloging in Publication Data:
Sarason, Donald.
    Sub-Hardy Hilbert spaces in the unit disk / Donald Sarason.
       p.   cm. — (The University of Arkansas lecture notes in the mathematical sciences; vol. 10)
    "A Wiley-Interscience publication."
    Includes bibliographical references and index.
    ISBN 0-471-04897-6
    1. Hilbert space. 2. Hardy spaces. I. Title. II. Series: University of Arkansas lecture notes in the mathematical sciences: v. 10.
QA322.4.S27   1995
515'.733—dc20   94-3410

Printed in the United States of America

10 9 8 7 6 5 4 3 2 1

FOREWORD

I have lived the greater part of my mathematical life in the unit disk of the complex plane. From afar the disk may seem a constraining environment, but to me, as to many predecessors, its terrain has offered unending fascination.

These notes focus on a family of Hilbert spaces that live inside the Hardy space H^2 of the disk. The spaces emerge from a viewpoint developed by Louis de Branges and were originally investigated around 1966 by de Branges in collaboration with James Rovnyak [14]. My own acquaintance with de Branges's viewpoint began, somewhat belatedly, with a 1984 lecture of his I heard. One of de Branges's key ideas is the notion of a complementary space, a generalization of the notion of orthogonal complement. In an effort to understand this notion I tried to see how it applies in a setting with which I was familiar, which took me back to the spaces of de Branges and Rovnyak. These spaces, and their vector-valued analogues, are the setting for the operator model theory of de Branges and Rovnyak [15]. My initial motivation was to understand the basic structure of the (scalar-valued) de Branges-Rovnyak spaces, and to understand the relation between the de Branges-Rovnyak model theory and the better known model theory of B. Sz.-Nagy and C. Foias (again, in the scalar-valued case). It soon became clear that, besides possessing a fascinating internal structure, the spaces of de Branges and Rovnyak have a role to play in several questions in function theory I had previously considered, and several additional ones as well. The aim of these notes is to describe some of what has been learned thus far about the structure of the de Branges–Rovnyak spaces and about their function-theoretic connections.

Chapter I introduces several Hilbert space notions, including that of a complementary space, needed in the sequel. The remaining chapters are devoted to an exploration of the structure of the spaces of de Branges and Rovnyak, which are introduced in Chapter II. There is one of these spaces associated with each nonconstant function b in the unit ball of H^∞; the space associated with b is denoted by $\mathcal{H}(b)$. A related space, denoted $\mathcal{H}(\bar{b})$, arises naturally in its study. The spaces $\mathcal{H}(b)$ and $\mathcal{H}(\bar{b})$ are invariant under the backward shift operator, and the restrictions of the backward shift to the spaces $\mathcal{H}(b)$ comprise the simplest class of de Branges-Rovnyak model operators.

In Chapter III, Cauchy integral representations of the spaces $\mathcal{H}(b)$ and $\mathcal{H}(\bar{b})$ are derived. In the case of $\mathcal{H}(b)$, the more complicated of the two cases, the representation gives an isometry between $\mathcal{H}(b)$ and the H^2 space of the measure on the unit circle whose Poisson integral is the real part of the function $\dfrac{1+b}{1-b}$.

The structures of $\mathcal{H}(b)$ and $\mathcal{H}(\bar{b})$ are sensitive in crucial ways to whether b is or is not an extreme point of the unit ball of H^∞. For example, these spaces are invariant under the forward shift operator if and only if b is not an extreme point. Chapter IV is devoted to the case where b is not an extreme point, and Chapter V to the case where it is an extreme point.

In Chapter VI it is shown that two classical theorems in function theory, C. Carathéodory's theorem on angular derivatives, and the theorem of A. Denjoy and J.Wolff on iteration, fit naturally within the context of the spaces $\mathcal{H}(b)$. Chapter VII sketches a partial extension of Carathéodory's theorem to higher derivatives.

Chapters VIII–X address a variety of questions concerning the spaces $\mathcal{H}(b)$ and $\mathcal{H}(\bar{b})$. For example, the conditions under which $\mathcal{H}(b)$ and $\mathcal{H}(\bar{b})$ coincide are determined, and the connection between $\mathcal{H}(b)$ and so-called rigid functions in H^1 is explained. The concluding Chapter XI contains brief mention of a few additional topics of current interest.

A large portion of the results presented here are already in the literature, and references to original sources are provided. Most references are confined to the Notes sections at the ends of most chapters. The treatment here, it is hoped, offers improvements over previous ones, thereby making the subject more accessible.

A preliminary version of these notes, under the title *Function Theory in the Unit Disk from a Hilbert Space Perspective*, was completed in 1991 and circulated to a few colleagues and students. That version has been revised to take account of recent developments and the comments of Wiley's reviewers. The author expresses his gratitude to the reviewers for their very helpful suggestions. He is also grateful to José Barría for detecting numerous corrections in the preliminary version. So as to avoid the task of renumbering the list of references, the references added after the completion of the preliminary version have been put in a supplementary list.

Besides possessing a standard background in real and complex analysis, functional analysis, and operator theory, the reader of these notes is assumed to be familiar with the theory of Hardy spaces in the unit disk. The material in the initial chapters of any of the standard references on Hardy spaces, such as the books of P. L. Duren [S2] and J. B. Garnett [27], will be adequate. Basic properties of Toeplitz operators will be needed from time to time. The book of R. G. Douglas [S1] is a good reference. Someone with the preceding prerequisites will find the treatment here reasonably self-contained.

These notes grew out of my 1989 lectures in the University of Arkansas Annual Lecture Series in the Mathematical Sciences. I am deeply indebted to the University of Arkansas for its splendid hospitality. Special thanks are due to the conference organizers: John Akeroyd, John Duncan, Daniel Luecking, Itrel Monroe, and William Summers.

Berkeley, California
December 22, 1993

CONTENTS

	Conventions	xi
	Index of Notations	xiii
I.	Hilbert Spaces Inside Hilbert Spaces	1
II.	Hilbert Spaces Inside H^2	9
III.	Cauchy Integral Representations	15
IV.	Nonextreme Points	23
V.	Extreme Points	37
VI.	Angular Derivatives	46
VII.	Higher Derivatives	58
VIII.	Equality of $\mathcal{H}(b)$ and $\mathcal{H}(\bar{b})$	60
IX.	Equality of $\mathcal{H}(b)$ and $\mathcal{M}(a)$	65
X.	Near Equality of $\mathcal{H}(b)$ and $\mathcal{M}(a)$	70
XI.	Brief Mention of a Few Additional Topics	81
	References	85
	Supplementary References	91
	Index	93

CONVENTIONS

The following standard conventions in notation and terminology are used in these notes.

1. All Hilbert spaces considered are assumed to be complex and separable.
2. Subspaces of a Hilbert space are assumed to be closed. The terms "vector subspace" and "linear manifold" are used to designate possibly nonclosed subspaces.
3. Hilbert space operators are assumed to be linear.
4. A scalar multiple of the identity operator on a Hilbert space is identified notationally with the corresponding scalar.
5. If H is a Hilbert space, then $\langle \cdot, \cdot \rangle_H$ and $\| \cdot \|_H$ denote the inner product and norm in H. The subscript will be modified in certain cases.
6. The open unit disk in the complex plane is denoted by D and its boundary, the unit circle, by ∂D.
7. L^p denotes the standard Lebesgue space with respect to normalized Lebesgue measure on ∂D. The corresponding Hardy space is denoted by H^p; in the usual way, it will be regarded either as a subspace of L^p or as a space of holomorphic functions in D, as convenience dictates. The space of functions in H^p that vanish at the origin is denoted by H_0^p. (The cases $p = 1, 2, \infty$ are the main ones of interest here.)
8. The inner product and norm in L^2 are denoted by $\langle \cdot, \cdot \rangle$ and $\| \cdot \|_2$.
9. The shift operator on H^2 is denoted by $S : (Sf)(z) = zf(z)$. It's adjoint, the backward shift, is given by $(S^*f)(z) = (f(z) - f(0))/z$.
10. If u and v are vectors in the Hilbert space H, then $u \otimes v$ denotes the rank-one operator on H that sends the vector x to the vector $\langle x, v \rangle_H u$.

INDEX OF NOTATIONS

The notations are listed in the order of appearance. Each is followed by the number of the section in which it is introduced.

$\mathcal{M}(A)$	I-2
$\mathcal{H}(A)$	I-4
T_φ	II-1
P_+	II-1
k_w	II-2
$\|\cdot\|_\varphi$	II-2
$\langle\cdot,\cdot\rangle_\varphi$	II-2
k_w^φ	II-2
b	II-2
$\mathcal{H}(b)$	II-2
$\mathcal{H}(\bar{b})$	II-2
X	II-7
Q_w	II-8
M_φ	II-10
$K\nu, K\sigma$	III-1
K_ν	III-1
$K^2(\nu)$	III-1
$H^2(\nu)$	III-1
$\langle\cdot,\cdot\rangle_\nu$	III-1
ρ	III-2
J_ρ	III-2
Z_ρ	III-3
μ	III-6
V_b	III-6
a	IV-1
h^+	IV-1

INDEX OF NOTATIONS

F	IV-9
F_λ	IV-9
μ_λ	IV-9
$H(D)$	IV-12
b_0	V-1
u_0	V-1
Y	IX-0
$\mathcal{H}_0(b)$	X-15
P_0	X-15
Y_0	X-15

SUB-HARDY HILBERT SPACES IN THE UNIT DISK

CHAPTER I

HILBERT SPACES INSIDE HILBERT SPACES

This chapter contains some general facts about Hilbert spaces and Hilbert space operators that are needed in the investigations to follow. The theme is Hilbert spaces that live inside larger Hilbert spaces. A Hilbert space contained boundedly in a larger Hilbert space can be realized as an operator range. The complementary space of an operator range is defined when the operator is a contraction. The approach to complementary spaces employed here emphasizes the operator viewpoint, whereas the original approach of de Branges is more geometric. The two approaches are reconciled in one of the notes at the end of the chapter.

A basic question one encounters in dealing with contained Hilbert spaces is that of recognizing when a given vector in the containing space also lies in the contained one. An often useful criterion will be given, which, for the complementary space associated with a given contraction, relates the question to the analogous one for the adjoint of the contraction.

Another basic issue is the relation between factorization of a contraction and decomposition of its associated complementary space. A general result along these lines will be established.

(I-1) Bounded and Contractive Containment. If H is a Hilbert space, one says that another Hilbert space is contained boundedly in H if it is a vector subspace of H and if the inclusion map of it into H is bounded. If the inclusion map is a contraction, one says that the second Hilbert space is contained contractively in H.

Examples come readily to mind. Every subspace of H is contained contractively (in fact, isometrically) in it. If H is somehow supplied with a second inner product giving an equivalent norm, then H equipped with the new inner product is contained boundedly in H equipped with the original one, and vice versa. If μ and ν are positive measures on the same sigma-algebra and μ dominates ν (i.e., is at least as large on every measurable set), then $L^2(\mu)$ is contained contractively in $L^2(\nu)$.

(I-2) Operator Ranges. If A is a bounded operator from the Hilbert space H_1 into the Hilbert space H, then we define $\mathcal{M}(A)$ to be the range of A with the Hilbert space structure that makes A a coisometry from H_1 onto $\mathcal{M}(A)$. Thus, if x and y are vectors in H_1 and if they are orthogonal to the kernel of A (or even if only one of them is orthogonal to the kernel of A), then

$$\langle Ax, Ay\rangle_{\mathcal{M}(A)} = \langle x, y\rangle_{H_1}.$$

The space $\mathcal{M}(A)$ is contained boundedly in H, and if A is a contraction it is contained contractively in H. Every Hilbert space contained boundedly in H is such an operator range; it is, namely, the range of the inclusion map of it into H.

(I-3) Transfer of Linear Functionals. Suppose H, H_1 and A have the meanings above, and let y be a vector in H. The restriction to $\mathcal{M}(A)$ of the linear functional on H induced by y is then a bounded linear functional on $\mathcal{M}(A)$. It is thus induced, relative to the inner product in $\mathcal{M}(A)$, by a vector in $\mathcal{M}(A)$. That vector is AA^*y, as one sees from the calculation

$$\langle Ax, y\rangle_H = \langle x, A^*y\rangle_{H_1} = \langle Ax, AA^*y\rangle_{\mathcal{M}(A)}.$$

(I-4) Douglas's Criterion. The following criterion of R. G. Douglas is often useful in establishing containment relations among spaces and in showing that an operator maps one space into another: *Let H, H_1 and H_2 be Hilbert spaces, and let A and B be bounded operators from H_1 and H_2, respectively, into H. Then the operator inequality $AA^* \leq BB^*$ is necessary and sufficient for the existence of a factorization $A = BR$ with R a contraction from H_1 into H_2.*

That the factorization implies the inequality is obvious. To establish the other half of the criterion one argues just as in the proof of the polar decomposition theorem. Namely, if the inequality holds, one first defines an operator Q from the range of B^* to the range of A^* by setting $QB^*x = A^*x$ ($x \in H$). The inequality implies that the definition makes sense and that Q does not increase norms. Thus Q extends by continuity to a contraction from the closure of the range of B^* into H_1. We can finally extend Q to a contraction from H_2 into H_1 by letting it be the zero operator on the orthogonal complement of the range of B^*. The operator $R = Q^*$ then has the desired properties.

(I-5) Consequences. The following conclusions are immediate consequences of Douglas's criterion.

(i) The space $\mathcal{M}(A)$ is contained contractively in the space $\mathcal{M}(B)$ if and only if $AA^* \leq BB^*$.

(ii) The spaces $\mathcal{M}(A)$ and $\mathcal{M}(B)$ coincide as Hilbert spaces if and only if $AA^* = BB^*$. In particular, $\mathcal{M}(A) = \mathcal{M}((AA^*)^{1/2})$.

(iii) The space $\mathcal{M}(A)$ is an ordinary subspace if and only if A is a partial isometry.

(I-6) Complementary Spaces. If A is a Hilbert space contraction, then the space $\mathcal{M}((1-AA^*)^{1/2})$ is called the complementary space of $\mathcal{M}(A)$ and is denoted by $\mathcal{H}(A)$. If $\mathcal{M}(A)$ is an ordinary subspace, in other words, if A is a partial isometry, then AA^* and $1 - AA^*$ are complementary projections, and $\mathcal{H}(A)$ is the ordinary orthogonal complement of $\mathcal{M}(A)$. In the contrary case the intersection $\mathcal{M}(A) \cap \mathcal{H}(A)$, called here an overlapping space, is nontrivial, as will be seen shortly.

(I-7) Intertwining Relation. *If A is a Hilbert space contraction, then* $A(1 - A^*A)^{1/2} = (1 - AA^*)^{1/2} A$.

The proof starts from the obvious equality $A(1 - A^*A) = (1 - AA^*)A$, which can be iterated to give $A(1 - A^*A)^n = (1 - AA^*)^n A$ for every positive integer n. Hence, if p is any polynomial, then $Ap(1 - A^*A) = p(1 - AA^*)A$. Now take a sequence $(p_n)_1^\infty$ of polynomials that converges uniformly on the interval $[0, 1]$ to the square-root function. Then $p_n(1 - A^*A) \to (1 - A^*A)^{1/2}$ in norm and $p_n(1 - AA^*) \to (1 - AA^*)^{1/2}$ in norm, and the desired equality follows.

(I-8) Relation Between $\mathcal{H}(A)$ and $\mathcal{H}(A^*)$. *Let A be a contraction from the Hilbert space H_1 into the Hilbert space H. Then the vector x in H belongs to $\mathcal{H}(A)$ if and only if A^*x belongs to $\mathcal{H}(A^*)$. If x_1 and x_2 are two vectors in $\mathcal{H}(A)$, then*

$$\langle x_1, x_2 \rangle_{\mathcal{H}(A)} = \langle x_1, x_2 \rangle_H + \langle A^*x_1, A^*x_2 \rangle_{\mathcal{H}(A^*)}.$$

In fact, the inclusion $A^*\mathcal{H}(A) \subset \mathcal{H}(A^*)$ follows immediately from the intertwining relation (I-7). Suppose on the other hand that x is a vector in H such that A^*x is in $\mathcal{H}(A^*)$, say $A^*x = (1 - A^*A)^{1/2}y$, where y is in H_1. Then the equality $x = (1 - AA^*)x + AA^*x$ can, in virtue of the intertwining relation, be rewritten as

$$x = (1 - AA^*)^{1/2}[(1 - AA^*)^{1/2}x + Ay],$$

which shows that x is in $\mathcal{H}(A)$.

To obtain the expression for the inner product, let x_1 and x_2 be two vectors in $\mathcal{H}(A)$, and for $j = 1, 2$ let y_j be the vector in H_1 that is orthogonal to the kernel of $1 - A^*A$ and satisfies $A^*x_j = (1 - A^*A)^{1/2}y_j$. For each j we then have

$$x_j = (1 - AA^*)^{1/2}[(1 - AA^*)^{1/2}x_j + Ay_j]$$

and, because of the way y_j was chosen, the vector in square brackets is orthogonal to the kernel of $1 - AA^*$, as one easily verifies. Hence

$$\langle x_1, x_2 \rangle_{\mathcal{H}(A)} = \langle (1 - AA^*)^{1/2}x_1 + Ay_1, (1 - AA^*)^{1/2}x_2 + Ay_2 \rangle_H.$$

When one expands the inner product on the right side one obtains four terms. One term is $\langle (1 - AA^*)^{1/2}x_1, (1 - AA^*)^{1/2}x_2 \rangle_H$, which is the same as $\langle x_1, x_2 \rangle_H - \langle A^*x_1, A^*x_2 \rangle_{H_1}$. Another is $\langle Ay_1, Ay_2 \rangle_H$. There are then two "cross-product" terms, of which one is $\langle (1 - AA^*)^{1/2}x_1, Ay_2 \rangle_H$. Because of the intertwining relation (I-7) this can be rewritten as

$$\langle A^*x_1, (1 - A^*A)^{1/2}y_2 \rangle_{H_1},$$

which equals $\langle A^*x_1, A^*x_2 \rangle_{H_1}$. The other cross-product term has the same value. All together, then, we have

$$\begin{aligned}\langle x_1, x_2 \rangle_{\mathcal{H}(A)} &= \langle x_1, x_2 \rangle_H + \langle A^*x_1, A^*x_2 \rangle_{H_1} + \langle Ay_1, Ay_2 \rangle_H \\ &= \langle x_1, x_2 \rangle_H + \langle (1 - A^*A)^{1/2}y_1, (1 - A^*A)^{1/2}y_2 \rangle_{H_1} + \langle Ay_1, Ay_2 \rangle_H \\ &= \langle x_1, x_2 \rangle_H + \langle y_1, y_2 \rangle_{H_1} \\ &= \langle x_1, x_2 \rangle_H + \langle A^*x_1, A^*x_2 \rangle_{\mathcal{H}(A^*)},\end{aligned}$$

as desired.

(I-9) Description of the Overlapping Space. *If A is as above, then $\mathcal{M}(A) \cap \mathcal{H}(A) = A\mathcal{H}(A^*)$.*

This follows immediately from (I-8) (with the roles of A and A^* reversed). Notice that the overlapping space is trivial if and only if $A(1 - A^*A)^{1/2} = 0$. If that happens then also $A(1 - A^*A) = 0$, so $A = AA^*A$. Then $AA^* = (AA^*)^2$, which means AA^* is a projection (that is, A is a partial isometry), and $\mathcal{M}(A)$ and $\mathcal{H}(A)$ are ordinary subspaces of H, orthogonal complements of each other.

(I-10) Factorizations of Operators and Decompositions of Spaces.
Let A be a contraction of the Hilbert space H_1 into the Hilbert space H. Suppose A has the factorization $A = A_2 A_1$ where A_2 is a contraction from the Hilbert space H_2 into H and A_1 is a contraction from H_1 into H_2. Then

$$\mathcal{H}(A) = \mathcal{H}(A_2) + A_2 \mathcal{H}(A_1).$$

If the vector x in $\mathcal{H}(A)$ is written as $x = x_2 + A_2 x_1$ with x_2 in $\mathcal{H}(A_2)$ and x_1 in $\mathcal{H}(A_1)$, then $\|x\|^2_{\mathcal{H}(A)} \leq \|x_2\|^2_{\mathcal{H}(A_2)} + \|x_1\|^2_{\mathcal{H}(A_1)}$. For each x there is a unique pair x_1, x_2 for which equality holds. The space $\mathcal{H}(A_2)$ is contained contractively in $\mathcal{H}(A)$, and the operator A_2 acts as a contraction from $\mathcal{H}(A_1)$ into $\mathcal{H}(A)$.

To establish this we rewrite the equality

$$1 - AA^* = 1 - A_2 A_2^* + A_2(1 - A_1 A_1^*)A_2^*$$

as $1 - AA^* = BB^*$, where $B = [B_1 \; B_2]$ is the operator from $H \oplus H_2$ to H given by $B_1 = (1 - A_2 A_2^*)^{1/2}$, $B_2 = A_2(1 - A_1 A_1^*)^{1/2}$. From (I-5)(ii) we see that $\mathcal{H}(A) = \mathcal{M}(B)$, from which the desired decomposition of $\mathcal{H}(A)$ follows immediately. To obtain the norm inequality, let x, x_2 and x_1 be as described, and let y_2 and y_1 be the vectors in H and H_2, respectively, that satisfy $x_j = (1 - A_j A_j^*)^{1/2} y_j$, and that are orthogonal to the kernels of $1 - A_2 A_2^*$ and $1 - A_1 A_1^*$, respectively. Then $x = B(y_2 \oplus y_1)$, so that

$$\|x\|^2_{\mathcal{H}(A)} \leq \|y_2\|^2_H + \|y_1\|^2_{H_2}$$
$$= \|x_2\|^2_{\mathcal{H}(A_2)} + \|x_1\|^2_{\mathcal{H}(A_1)},$$

as desired. Moreover, equality holds here if and only if $y_2 \oplus y_1$ happens to be the unique vector orthogonal to the kernel of B such that $x = B(y_2 \oplus y_1)$. From this one sees that there is a unique pair x_1, x_2 for which equality holds. Finally, it is an immediate consequence of the norm inequality that $\mathcal{H}(A_2)$ is contained contractively in $\mathcal{H}(A)$ and that A_2 acts as a contraction of $\mathcal{H}(A_1)$ into $\mathcal{H}(A)$.

(I-11) Orthogonal Decompositions. Retaining the notations of (I-10) we note that the condition that the decomposition $\mathcal{H}(A) = \mathcal{H}(A_2) + A_2 \mathcal{H}(A_1)$ be an algebraic direct sum, namely, the triviality of the intersection $\mathcal{H}(A_2) \cap A_2 \mathcal{H}(A_1)$, is exactly the condition that the kernel of B split into the direct sum of the kernels of B_1 and B_2. If that happens then the decomposition above is an orthogonal direct sum (relative to the inner product in $\mathcal{H}(A)$), and $\mathcal{H}(A_2)$ is contained isometrically in $\mathcal{H}(A)$. Furthermore, it is asserted, the operator A_2 then acts as a partial isometry of $\mathcal{H}(A_1)$ into $\mathcal{H}(A)$. To prove this, suppose the vector u in $\mathcal{H}(A_1)$ is orthogonal to $\ker A_2 \cap \mathcal{H}(A_1)$, relative to the inner product in $\mathcal{H}(A_1)$, and write $u = (1 - A_1 A_1^*)^{1/2} v$ with v in H_2 and orthogonal to the kernel of $1 - A_1 A_1^*$ (so that $\|u\|_{\mathcal{H}(A_1)} = \|v\|_{H_2}$). The equality $\|A_2 u\|_{\mathcal{H}(A)} = \|u\|_{\mathcal{H}(A_1)}$ will then follow if v is orthogonal to the kernel of $A_2(1 - A_1 A_1^*)^{1/2}$ (since that will mean $\|A_2 u\|_{\mathcal{H}(A)} = \|v\|_{H_2}$). Thus, suppose the vector w belongs to the kernel of $A_2(1 - A_1 A_1^*)^{1/2}$. Then $(1 - A_1 A_1^*)^{1/2} w$ belongs to $\ker A_2 \cap \mathcal{H}(A_1)$, implying that

$$\begin{aligned} 0 &= \langle u, (1 - A_1 A_1^*)^{1/2} w \rangle_{\mathcal{H}(A_1)} \\ &= \langle (1 - A_1 A_1^*)^{1/2} v, (1 - A_1 A_1^*)^{1/2} w \rangle_{\mathcal{H}(A_1)} \\ &= \langle v, w \rangle_{H_2}, \end{aligned}$$

the desired conclusion.

(I-12) Decomposition of the Underlying Space. Suppose A is a contraction of the Hilbert space H_1 into the Hilbert space H, and consider the factorization $0 = A0$, where on the left side we have the zero operator of H_1 into H and on the right side the zero operator of H_1 into itself. The decomposition from (I-10) then reduces to

$$H = \mathcal{H}(A) + \mathcal{M}(A).$$

Moreover, the norm inequality tells us that if x is in H and $x = x_2 + A x_1$ with x_2 in $\mathcal{H}(A)$ and x_1 in H_1, then $\|x\|_H^2 \leq \|x_2\|_{\mathcal{H}(A)}^2 + \|x_1\|_{H_1}^2$. The vectors x_1 and x_2 that yield equality are easily determined, for in the present case the operator B used in the proof of (I-10) has first component $B_1 = (1 - AA^*)^{1/2}$ and second component $B_2 = A$. One easily checks that B^* is an isometry, so its range is the orthogonal complement of the kernel of B. Thus, to obtain equality one must take for x_2 the image under B_1 of the first component of $B^* x$ and for x_1 the second component of $B^* x$, in other words, $x_2 = (1 - AA^*)x$ and $x_1 = A^* x$.

Notes

(NI-1) The notion of a complementary space was introduced, in the context of square-summable power series, by L. de Branges and J. Rovnyak in their book [14] and paper [15]. The kernel of the idea can be detected in the fundamental paper [6] of N. Aronszajn. de Branges's forthcoming book [13] contains a treatment in the abstract context employed here. As will be explained below, in (NI-6), the definition used by de Branges and Rovnyak is different from but equivalent to the one used here.

(NI-2) The ideas of contractive containment and complementary space were critical in de Branges's discovery of his proof of the Bieberbach conjecture [12]. Although a proof of the conjecture that expunges these ideas can be given, and such a proof might seem preferable to specialists in geometric function theory, the role of Hilbert space ideas is really very natural, as is made manifest by the study [53] of V. I. Vasyunin and N. K. Nikolskii, which further develops de Branges's approach.

(NI-3) Douglas's criterion (I-4) can be found in [22].

(NI-4) The intertwining relation (I-7), which plays a basic role in the theory of unitary dilations, comes from the first paper on that subject, P. R. Halmos's paper [28].

(NI-5) Proposition (I-8) on the relation between $\mathcal{H}(A)$ and $\mathcal{H}(A^*)$ is taken from the paper [44] of B. A. Lotto and the author.

(NI-6) Suppose A is a contraction from the Hilbert space H_1 into the Hilbert space H. The result in (I-12), slightly rephrased, says that if x is in $\mathcal{H}(A)$ and y is in $\mathcal{M}(A)$, then

$$\|x\|^2_{\mathcal{H}(A)} \geq \|x+y\|^2_H - \|y\|^2_{\mathcal{M}(A)},$$

with equality only in case $(1 - AA^*)y = AA^*x$. If x happens to belong to the range of $1 - AA^*$ then there is a y in $\mathcal{M}(A)$ for which equality holds; thus, the equality is attainable for a dense set in $\mathcal{H}(A)$. It follows that the norm of any vector x in $\mathcal{H}(A)$ is given by

$$\|x\|^2_{\mathcal{H}(A)} = \sup_{y \in \mathcal{M}(A)} (\|x+y\|^2_H - \|y\|^2_{\mathcal{M}(A)}),$$

which leads us to the definition of complementary space used by de Branges and Rovnyak. Given a Hilbert space $\mathcal{M}$ contained contractively in H, they define its complementary space to be the space of vectors x in H such that

$$\sup_{y \in \mathcal{M}} (\|x + y\|_H^2 - \|y\|_{\mathcal{M}}^2) < \infty,$$

with the norm given by the square root of the preceding supremum.

To see that the de Branges–Rovnyak definition of complementary space is equivalent to the one used here it only remains to show that, with A as above, if x is in H and

$$c = \sup_{y_1 \in H_1} (\|x + Ay_1\|_H^2 - \|y_1\|_{H_1}^2) < \infty,$$

then x is in $\mathcal{H}(A)$. Assume x satisfies the preceding condition. We can rewrite the condition as

$$\|(1 - A^*A)^{1/2} y_1\|_{H_1}^2 - 2\operatorname{Re}\langle A^*x, y_1\rangle_{H_1} + c - \|x\|_H^2 \geq 0,$$

which is supposed to hold for all y_1 in H_1. We shall show that this implies that A^*x is in $\mathcal{H}(A^*)$, and hence by (I-8) that x is in $\mathcal{H}(A)$. Replacing y_1 by ty_1 (t a real variable) in the inequality above, we obtain

$$t^2 \|(1 - A^*A)^{1/2} y_1\|_{H_1}^2 - 2t \operatorname{Re}\langle A^*x, y_1\rangle_{H_1} + c - \|x\|_H^2 \geq 0,$$

from which it follows that

$$|\operatorname{Re}\langle A^*x, y_1\rangle_{H_1}| \leq (c - \|x\|_H^2)^{1/2} \|(1 - A^*A)^{1/2} y_1\|_{H_1}.$$

This being true for all y_1 in H_1, we can conclude that

$$|\langle A^*x, y_1\rangle_{H_1}| \leq (c - \|x\|_H^2)^{1/2} \|(1 - A^*A)^{1/2} y_1\|_{H_1}$$

for all y_1 in H_1. That this inequality implies A^*x is in the range of $(1 - A^*A)^{1/2}$ is easily deduced from the spectral theorem. A proof in the spirit of the present work goes as follows. Rewriting the inequality as

$$|\langle A^*x, y_1\rangle_{H_1}| \leq (c - \|x\|_H^2)^{1/2} \|(1 - A^*A) y_1\|_{\mathcal{H}(A^*)},$$

we see that the map $(1 - A^*A)y_1 \to \langle A^*x, y_1\rangle_{H_1}$ defines a bounded conjugate linear functional on (a dense linear manifold in) $\mathcal{H}(A^*)$. There is therefore a vector x_1 in $\mathcal{H}(A^*)$ such that $\langle A^*x, y_1\rangle_{H_1} = \langle x_1, (1 - A^*A)y_1\rangle_{\mathcal{H}(A^*)}$ for all y_1 in H_1. Since $\langle x_1, (1 - A^*A)y_1\rangle_{\mathcal{H}(A^*)} = \langle x_1, y_1\rangle_{H_1}$, we must have $A^*x = x_1$.

(NI-7) The term "overlapping space" is used by the de Branges school in a slightly different way than it is used here.

CHAPTER II

HILBERT SPACES INSIDE H^2

The spaces that are to be our main concern will now be introduced. They emerge from the scheme in Chapter I when the operators of concern are Toeplitz operators on the Hardy space H^2 of the unit disk. As mentioned in the foreword, there is associated with each nonconstant function b in the unit ball of H^∞ a pair of these spaces, denoted $\mathcal{H}(b)$ and $\mathcal{H}(\overline{b})$, the former of which is the primary focus of this study. After the spaces have been defined, a few of their properties that follow easily from results in Chapter I will be deduced. The kernel functions for $\mathcal{H}(b)$ will be identified, and the relation between $\mathcal{H}(b)$ and $\mathcal{H}(\overline{b})$ will be explicated. It will be shown that $\mathcal{H}(b)$ and $\mathcal{H}(\overline{b})$ are both invariant under conjugate-analytic Toeplitz operators. That enables one, in particular, to exhibit a supply of functions that belong to $\mathcal{H}(b)$. The adjoint of the restriction to $\mathcal{H}(b)$ of the backward shift will be identified, and some general remarks about multipliers of $\mathcal{H}(b)$ will be made.

(II-1) Toeplitz Operators. For φ a function in L^∞ of the unit circle, T_φ will denote the Toeplitz operator on H^2 with symbol φ. It is given by $T_\varphi f = P_+(\varphi f)$, where P_+ is the orthogonal projection in L^2 with range H^2. Only simple properties of Toeplitz operators will be needed. Here are three:

(i) $\|T_\varphi\| = \|\varphi\|_\infty$
(ii) $T_\varphi^* = T_{\overline{\varphi}}$
(iii) If φ and ψ are in L^∞ and at least one of them is in H^∞, then $T_{\overline{\psi}} T_\varphi = T_{\overline{\psi}\varphi}$.

We shall denote the space $\mathcal{M}(T_\varphi)$ by $\mathcal{M}(\varphi)$. If $\|\varphi\|_\infty \leq 1$, we denote the space $\mathcal{H}(T_\varphi)$ by $\mathcal{H}(\varphi)$. The norm and inner product in $\mathcal{H}(\varphi)$ will be denoted by $\|\cdot\|_\varphi$ and $\langle \cdot, \cdot \rangle_\varphi$.

For w in D, we let k_w denote the kernel function for the functional on H^2 of evaluation at w; it is given by $k_w(z) = (1 - \overline{w}z)^{-1}$ and is defined by the property $f(w) = \langle f, k_w \rangle$ ($f \in H^2$). If φ is in L^∞ and $\|\varphi\|_\infty \leq 1$, we let

k_w^φ denote the kernel function for the functional on $\mathcal{H}(\varphi)$ of evaluation at w. From (I-3) one sees that $k_w^\varphi = (1 - T_\varphi T_{\overline{\varphi}})k_w$.

(II-2) de Branges–Rovnyak Spaces. From now on, b will denote a nonconstant function in the unit ball of H^∞. Our aim is to understand the structure of the space $\mathcal{H}(b)$ and (to the extent needed for this) the structure of its cousin, $\mathcal{H}(\overline{b})$. The operator inequality $T_b T_{\overline{b}} \leq T_{\overline{b}} T_b$, in conjunction with (I-5)(i), implies that $\mathcal{H}(\overline{b})$ is contained contractively in $\mathcal{H}(b)$.

The space $\mathcal{H}(b)$ is an ordinary subspace of H^2 if and only if T_b is a partial isometry. That happens if and only if b is an inner function (so T_b is actually an isometry). Then $\mathcal{H}(b)$ is the orthogonal complement of the Beurling invariant subspace bH^2, the typical nontrivial invariant subspace of the shift operator, S. Hence, the spaces $\mathcal{H}(b)$ with b inner are the nontrivial invariant subspaces of the backward shift, S^*. If b is inner then $\mathcal{H}(\overline{b})$ is trivial, but otherwise, as one easily sees, $\mathcal{H}(\overline{b})$ is infinite dimensional.

At the other extreme is the case where $\|b\|_\infty < 1$. Then $\mathcal{H}(b)$ is just a renormed version of H^2.

(II-3) Kernel Function for $\mathcal{H}(b)$. For w a point of D we have, as noted in (II-1), $k_w^b = (1 - T_b T_{\overline{b}})k_w$. Since $T_{\overline{b}} k_w = \overline{b(w)} k_w$, one obtains the expression $k_w^b = (1 - \overline{b(w)} b)k_w$. In particular,

$$\|k_w^b\|_b^2 = k_w^b(w) = \frac{1 - |b(w)|^2}{1 - |w|^2}.$$

(II-4) Relation Between $\mathcal{H}(b)$ and $\mathcal{H}(\overline{b})$. From (I-8) one concludes that the H^2 function h belongs to $\mathcal{H}(b)$ if and only if $T_{\overline{b}} h$ belongs to $\mathcal{H}(\overline{b})$. Moreover, if h_1 and h_2 are two functions in $\mathcal{H}(b)$, then

$$\langle h_1, h_2 \rangle_b = \langle h_1, h_2 \rangle + \langle T_{\overline{b}} h_1, T_{\overline{b}} h_2 \rangle_{\overline{b}}.$$

(II-5) Overlapping Space of $\mathcal{H}(b)$ and $\mathcal{M}(b)$. By (I-9), the overlapping space $\mathcal{H}(b) \cap \mathcal{M}(b)$ equals $T_b \mathcal{H}(\overline{b})$.

(II-6) Effect of an Inner Factor. By (I-10) and (I-11), if u is an inner function then $\mathcal{H}(ub)$ is the orthogonal direct sum of $\mathcal{H}(u)$ and $T_u \mathcal{H}(b)$. The space $\mathcal{H}(u)$ is contained isometrically in $\mathcal{H}(ub)$, and T_u acts as an isometry of $\mathcal{H}(b)$ into $\mathcal{H}(ub)$.

(II-7) Invariance Under Conjugate–Analytic Toeplitz Operators.
If φ is in H^∞, then $\mathcal{H}(b)$ and $\mathcal{H}(\bar{b})$ are both invariant under $T_{\bar{\varphi}}$, and the norm of $T_{\bar{\varphi}}$ as an operator in each of these spaces does not exceed $\|\varphi\|_\infty$.

In proving this we can assume without loss of generality that $\|\varphi\|_\infty = 1$. By Douglas's criterion (I-4), to show that $T_{\bar{\varphi}}$ acts as a contraction in $\mathcal{H}(\bar{b})$ it is enough to verify the inequality

$$T_\varphi(1 - T_{\bar{b}}T_b)T_{\bar{\varphi}} \leq 1 - T_{\bar{b}}T_b.$$

The difference between the operator on the right side in this inequality and the operator on the left side is

$$1 - T_{|b|^2} - T_{|\varphi|^2} + T_{|\varphi b|^2},$$

which is the Toeplitz operator with symbol $(1 - |\varphi|^2)(1 - |b|^2)$, hence positive semidefinite (in fact positive definite unless the symbol vanishes). The inequality therefore holds, which settles the proposition for $\mathcal{H}(\bar{b})$.

Because of (II-4), the proposition for $\mathcal{H}(b)$ can be reduced to the proposition for $\mathcal{H}(\bar{b})$. Let h be a function in $\mathcal{H}(b)$. Since $T_{\bar{b}}T_{\bar{\varphi}}h = T_{\bar{\varphi}}T_{\bar{b}}h$, the function $T_{\bar{b}}T_{\bar{\varphi}}h$ belongs to $\mathcal{H}(\bar{b})$ by (II-4) and what was just proved. And since it is in $\mathcal{H}(\bar{b})$, it follows from (II-4) that $T_{\bar{\varphi}}h$ is in $\mathcal{H}(b)$, as desired. Moreover

$$\|T_{\bar{\varphi}}h\|_b^2 = \|T_{\bar{\varphi}}h\|_2^2 + \|T_{\bar{\varphi}}T_{\bar{b}}h\|_{\bar{b}}^2$$
$$\leq \|h\|_2^2 + \|T_{\bar{b}}h\|_{\bar{b}}^2 = \|h\|_b^2,$$

so $T_{\bar{\varphi}}$ acts as a contraction in $\mathcal{H}(b)$. This completes the proof.

In particular, then, the space $\mathcal{H}(b)$ is invariant under the operator S^*, which acts as a contraction in $\mathcal{H}(b)$. Henceforth the restriction $S^*|\mathcal{H}(b)$ will be denoted by X.

(II-8) More Inhabitants of $\mathcal{H}(b)$. Up to now our only explicit examples of functions in $\mathcal{H}(b)$ have been the kernel functions, k_w^b. The preceding proposition provides a few more examples.

We first show that S^*b belongs to $\mathcal{H}(b)$. We have

$$T_{\bar{b}}S^*b = S^*T_{\bar{b}}b = -S^*(1 - T_{\bar{b}}T_b)1.$$

The function $(1 - T_{\bar{b}}T_b)1$ belongs to $\mathcal{H}(\bar{b})$, thus so does $T_{\bar{b}}S^*b$, by (II-7). Therefore S^*b is in $\mathcal{H}(b)$, by (II-4).

Does b itself belong to $\mathcal{H}(b)$? That question will be answered later, in Chapters IV and V.

For w in D, define the operator Q_w on H^2 by $(Q_w f)(z) = \dfrac{f(z) - f(w)}{z - w}$; in particular, $Q_0 = S^*$. The alternative expression $Q_w = (1 - wS^*)^{-1} S^*$ is easily verified. In particular, then, $Q_w b = (1 - wX)^{-1} S^* b$, showing that all the functions $Q_w b$ belong to $\mathcal{H}(b)$.

(II-9) The Adjoint of X. *For h in $\mathcal{H}(b)$,*

$$X^* h = Sh - \langle h, S^* b \rangle_b b.$$

In fact, for w in D we have

$$(X^* h)(w) = \langle X^* h, k_w^b \rangle_b = \langle h, X k_w^b \rangle_b.$$

Using the formula $k_w^b = (1 - \overline{b(w)} b) k_w$ from (II-3) and the identity $S^*(fg) = f S^* g + g(0) S^* f$, one finds that $S^* k_w^b = \overline{w} k_w^b - \overline{b(w)} S^* b$. This together with the preceding equality gives

$$\begin{aligned}(X^* h)(w) &= w \langle h, k_w^b \rangle_b - b(w) \langle h, S^* b \rangle_b \\ &= w h(w) - \langle h, S^* b \rangle_b b(w),\end{aligned}$$

as desired.

(II-10) Multipliers. A function φ in H^∞ is called a multiplier of $\mathcal{H}(b)$ if $\mathcal{H}(b)$ is invariant under T_φ. Multipliers of $\mathcal{H}(\bar{b})$ are defined analogously. The equality $\mathcal{H}(b) \cap \mathcal{M}(b) = T_b \mathcal{H}(\bar{b})$ from (II-5) implies that every multiplier of $\mathcal{H}(b)$ is a multiplier of $\mathcal{H}(\bar{b})$.

If φ is a multiplier of $\mathcal{H}(b)$, we denote the restriction of T_φ to $\mathcal{H}(b)$ by M_φ. It is a bounded operator, by the closed graph theorem. For w a point of D, the range of the operator $M_\varphi - \varphi(w)$ is orthogonal to the kernel function k_w^b, implying that k_w^b is an eigenvector of M_φ^* with eigenvalue $\overline{\varphi(w)}$.

Conversely, if M is a bounded operator on $\mathcal{H}(b)$ such that each kernel function k_w^b is an eigenvector of M^*, then M is the multiplication operator induced by a multiplier of $\mathcal{H}(b)$. To see this, let $\varphi(w)$ denote the complex conjugate of the eigenvalue of k_w^b as an eigenvector of M^*. Then for h in $\mathcal{H}(b)$ and w in D we have

$$\begin{aligned}Mh(w) &= \langle Mh, k_w^b \rangle_b = \langle h, M^* k_w^b \rangle_b \\ &= \varphi(w) \langle h, k_w^b \rangle_b = \varphi(w) h(w),\end{aligned}$$

which implies that φ is holomorphic and that M is the multiplication operator induced by φ. To see that φ is bounded one notes that

$$\|M\|^2 \|k_w^b\|_b^2 \geq \|M^* k_w^b\|_b^2 = |\varphi(w)|^2 \|k_w^b\|_b^2;$$

hence $\|\varphi\|_\infty \leq \|M\|$.

We note for future reference that if φ is a multiplier of $\mathcal{H}(b)$ then so is $Q_w \varphi$ for every w in D. This follows from the easily established identity

$$(Q_w \varphi)h = Q_w(\varphi h) - \varphi(w) Q_w h.$$

Notes

(NII-1) The spaces $\mathcal{H}(b)$ were introduced and studied by de Branges and Rovnyak in their book [14]. Subsequent work has been done by the author [58], [59], [60], [62], [63], B. A. Lotto [43], Lotto and the author [44], and B. M. Davis and J. E. McCarthy [20].

(NII-2) The vector-valued versions of $\mathcal{H}(b)$, first investigated by de Branges and Rovnyak [15], are important in the theory of model operators. A penetrating study of them was made by J. A. Ball in his dissertation [7]. The dissertation was never published as such, but many of its ideas appear in subsequent papers authored or jointly authored by Ball. There has been a great deal of more recent work, for example by Ball and A. Lubin [10], Ball and T. L. Kriete [9], Ball and N. Cohen [8], Nikolskii and Vasyunin [51], [52], H. Dym [24], D. Alpay and Dym [4], [5], and de Branges [13].

(NII-3) The connection made in (II-10) between multiplication operators on $\mathcal{H}(b)$ and operators on $\mathcal{H}(b)$ having the kernel functions k_w^b as eigenvectors is a general property of reproducing kernel Hilbert spaces. More information can be found in the paper [64] of A. L. Shields and L. J. Wallen.

CHAPTER III

CAUCHY INTEGRAL REPRESENTATIONS

The spaces $\mathcal{H}(b)$ and $\mathcal{H}(\bar{b})$ turn out to be transforms, via Cauchy integrals, of weighted H^2 spaces. For $\mathcal{H}(\bar{b})$, the simpler of the two cases, the H^2 space is that of the weight $\rho = 1 - |b|^2$. For $\mathcal{H}(b)$ it is the H^2 space of the measure μ on ∂D whose Poisson integral is the real part of the function $\dfrac{1+b}{1-b}$. In each case, the operator on the weighted H^2 space that transforms into the restricted backward shift is easily determined: for $\mathcal{H}(\bar{b})$ it is the adjoint of the operator on $H^2(\rho)$ of multiplication by the independent variable, and for $\mathcal{H}(b)$ it is a rank-one perturbation of the analogous operator on $H^2(\mu)$. For $\mathcal{H}(\bar{b})$, the preceding statement generalizes to all restricted conjugate-analytic Toeplitz operators. For $\mathcal{H}(b)$ there is a similar result, not for restricted conjugate-analytic Toeplitz operators, but for the adjoints of multiplication operators.

Given b and another function, u, in the unit ball of H^∞, with corresponding measure ν (bearing the same relation to u as μ does to b), how can one determine, by looking only at b and u, whether ν is absolutely continuous with respect to μ? This question, besides being a natural one in its own right, comes up in connection with several others. The simplest case is where ν is a point mass; the question then relates to the existence for b of an angular derivative in the sense of Carathéodory, to be discussed in Chapter VI. A criterion for absolute continuity involving $\mathcal{H}(b)$ will be obtained in this chapter; it pertains to the case where the measure ν is singular with respect to Lebesgue measure on ∂D (or, what is equivalent, to the case where u is an inner function). The criterion will be refined in Chapters IV and V.

(III-1) **Cauchy Integrals.** For ν a complex Borel measure on ∂D, the Cauchy integral of ν is the holomorphic function $K\nu$ defined in $\mathbb{C}\backslash\partial D$ by

$$K\nu(z) = \int_{\partial D} \frac{1}{1 - e^{-i\theta}z} d\nu(e^{i\theta}).$$

If ν is absolutely continuous and σ is its Radon–Nikodym derivative with respect to normalized Lebesgue measure, we write $K\sigma$ in place of $K\nu$. Notice that if σ is in L^2 then $P_+\sigma = K\sigma|D$.

If ν is a positive measure and q is a function in $L^2(\nu)$, we let

$$K_\nu q = K(q\nu)|D,$$

and we think of K_ν as an operator on $L^2(\nu)$. The space of functions into which K_ν transforms $L^2(\nu)$ will be denoted by $K^2(\nu)$. (As before, if ν is absolutely continuous with normalized Radon–Nikodym derivative σ, we write K_σ and $K^2(\sigma)$ in place of K_ν and $K^2(\nu)$.) Denoting the inner product in $L^2(\nu)$ by $\langle \cdot, \cdot \rangle_\nu$, we can thus write, for z in D,

$$K_\nu q(z) = \langle q, k_z \rangle_\nu.$$

Hence, the kernel of K_ν is the orthogonal complement of the span in $L^2(\nu)$ of the kernel functions k_z ($z \in D$), and it is easily seen that this span coincides with $H^2(\nu)$, the closure of the polynomials in $L^2(\nu)$.

(III-2) Representation of $\mathcal{H}(\bar{b})$. Let ρ denote the function $1 - |b|^2$ on ∂D. (This notation will remain fixed.) If q is a function in $L^2(\rho)$ then $q\rho$ is in L^2, being the product of the L^2 function $q\rho^{1/2}$ and the bounded function $\rho^{1/2}$. That implies $K_\rho q \ (= P_+(\rho q))$ is in H^2. We are thus entitled to think of K_ρ as an operator from $L^2(\rho)$ into H^2, and the adjoint of that operator is the natural injection of H^2 into $L^2(\rho)$, as one sees from the obvious string of equalities

$$\langle K_\rho q, f \rangle = \langle P_+(\rho q), f \rangle = \langle \rho q, f \rangle$$
$$= \langle q, f \rangle_\rho \qquad (q \in L^2(\rho),\ f \in H^2).$$

We shall denote the injection of H^2 into $L^2(\rho)$ by J_ρ. The equality $K_\rho J_\rho = T_\rho$ holds in virtue of another obvious string of equalities:

$$\langle K_\rho J_\rho f, g \rangle = \langle J_\rho f, J_\rho g \rangle_\rho = \langle \rho f, g \rangle$$
$$= \langle T_\rho f, g \rangle \qquad (f, g \in H^2).$$

But $T_\rho = 1 - T_{\bar{b}}T_b$, so it follows by (I-5)(ii) that $\mathcal{H}(\bar{b}) = \mathcal{M}(K_\rho)\ (= K^2(\rho))$. Thus, since the kernel of K_ρ is the orthogonal complement of $H^2(\rho)$, the transformation K_ρ is an isometry of $H^2(\rho)$ onto $\mathcal{H}(b)$. From (I-3) we have $k_w^{\bar{b}} = K_\rho k_w$ ($w \in D$).

(III-3) An Intertwining Relation. The operator on $H^2(\rho)$ of multiplication by the independent variable will be denoted by Z_ρ ($Z_\rho q(e^{i\theta}) = e^{i\theta}q(e^{i\theta})$). We then have the relation $K_\rho Z_\rho^* = S^* K_\rho$. In fact, if q is in $L^2(\rho)$ then, for z in D,

$$K_\rho Z_\rho^* q(z) = \langle Z_\rho^* q, k_z \rangle_\rho = \langle q, Z_\rho k_z \rangle_\rho$$
$$= \frac{1}{2\pi} \int_{\partial D} \frac{e^{-i\theta} q(e^{i\theta}) \rho(e^{i\theta})}{1 - e^{-i\theta} z} d\theta.$$

That the right side equals $S^* K_\rho q(z)$ follows by a trivial calculation which, for future reference, will be done in greater generality.

(III-4) Backward Shifts of Cauchy Integrals. *If ν is a complex Borel measure on ∂D, then*

$$\int_{\partial D} \frac{e^{-i\theta}}{1 - e^{-i\theta} z} d\nu(e^{i\theta}) = \frac{K\nu(z) - K\nu(0)}{z} \qquad (z \in \mathbb{C} \backslash \partial D,\ z \neq 0).$$

To prove this it suffices to note that

$$\frac{e^{-i\theta}}{1 - e^{-i\theta} z} = \frac{1}{z}\left[\frac{1}{1 - e^{-i\theta} z} - 1\right].$$

(III-5) More Intertwining. *If φ is in H^∞, then $K_\rho \varphi(Z_\rho)^* = T_{\overline{\varphi}} K_\rho$.*

In fact, the case where φ is a polynomial follows immediately from (III-3). To obtain the general case it suffices to take a sequence of polynomials that is uniformly bounded on ∂D and converges almost everywhere to φ, and then to apply a standard limit argument.

(III-6) The Measure μ. Since the harmonic function $\operatorname{Re}\left(\dfrac{1+b}{1-b}\right)$ is positive, it is the Poisson integral of a positive measure on ∂D, which we shall denote by μ. (The notation will remain fixed. All positive Borel measures on ∂D of course arise in this way.) We thus have the Herglotz integral representation

$$\frac{1 + b(z)}{1 - b(z)} = \int_{\partial D} \frac{e^{i\theta} + z}{e^{i\theta} - z} d\mu(e^{i\theta}) + i \operatorname{Im} \frac{1 + b(0)}{1 - b(0)}.$$

As the first and main step in establishing the Cauchy integral representation of $\mathcal{H}(b)$, we compute $\langle k_w, k_z \rangle_\mu$ for two points z and w in D:

$$\langle k_w, k_z \rangle_\mu = \int_{\partial D} \frac{1}{(1 - e^{i\theta}\overline{w})(1 - e^{-i\theta}z)} d\mu(e^{i\theta})$$

$$= \frac{1}{1 - \overline{w}z} \int_{\partial D} \frac{1}{2} \left[\frac{e^{-i\theta} + \overline{w}}{e^{-i\theta} - \overline{w}} + \frac{e^{i\theta} + z}{e^{i\theta} - z} \right] d\mu(e^{i\theta})$$

$$= \frac{1}{2(1 - \overline{w}z)} \left[\frac{1 + \overline{b(w)}}{1 - \overline{b(w)}} + \frac{1 + b(z)}{1 - b(z)} \right]$$

$$= \frac{1 - \overline{b(w)}b(z)}{(1 - \overline{b(w)})(1 - b(z))(1 - \overline{w}z)}$$

$$= (1 - \overline{b(w)})^{-1}(1 - b(z))^{-1} k_w^b(z)$$

$$= \langle (1 - \overline{b(w)})^{-1} k_w^b, (1 - \overline{b(z)})^{-1} k_z^b \rangle_b.$$

We now define the transformation V_b on $L^2(\mu)$ by $V_b q(z) = (1-b(z))K_\mu q(z)$ ($z \in D$).

(III-7) Representation of $\mathcal{H}(b)$. *The transformation V_b is an isometry of $H^2(\mu)$ onto $\mathcal{H}(b)$.*

In fact, the preceding calculation shows that $V_b k_w = (1 - \overline{b(w)})^{-1} k_w^b$, and that $\langle k_w, k_z \rangle_\mu = \langle V_b k_w, V_b k_z \rangle_b$. The transformation V_b thus maps the linear span of the functions k_w (a dense linear manifold in $H^2(\mu)$) onto the linear span of the functions k_w^b (a dense linear manifold in $\mathcal{H}(b)$), and the map is isometric relative to the norms in $H^2(\mu)$ and $\mathcal{H}(b)$. A standard limit argument completes the proof.

(III-8) An Intertwining Relation. Let Z_μ denote the operator on $H^2(\mu)$ of multiplication by the independent variable. To determine how Z_μ^* is transformed under V_b, we use (III-4) to get, for q in $H^2(\mu)$,

$$V_b Z_\mu^* q(z) = (1 - b(z)) K_\mu Z_\mu^* q(z)$$
$$= (1 - b(z)) \left(\frac{K_\mu q(z) - K_\mu q(0)}{z} \right),$$

which can be written
$$V_b Z_\mu^* q = S^* V_b q + K_\mu q(0) S^* b.$$
In particular,
$$V_b Z_\mu^* 1 = (1 - \overline{b(0)})^{-1} S^* k_0^b + \|\mu\| S^* b.$$
Since $k_0^b = 1 - \overline{b(0)} b$ and $\|\mu\| = \operatorname{Re} \dfrac{1 + b(0)}{1 - b(0)} = \dfrac{1 - |b(0)|^2}{|1 - b(0)|^2}$, this reduces to
$$V_b Z_\mu^* 1 = \left[\frac{-\overline{b(0)}}{1 - \overline{b(0)}} + \frac{1 - |b(0)|^2}{|1 - b(0)|^2} \right] S^* b$$
$$= (1 - b(0))^{-1} S^* b.$$
Returning to the formula for $V_b Z_\mu^* q$, we can now rewrite it as
$$V_b Z_\mu^* q = X V_b q + \langle q, 1 \rangle_\mu S^* b$$
$$= X V_b q + (1 - b(0)) \langle q, 1 \rangle_\mu V_b Z_\mu^* 1.$$
It follows that
$$X V_b = V_b Z_\mu^* (1 \quad (1 - b(0))(1 \otimes 1)).$$
An alternative expression is
$$V_b Z_\mu^* V_b^{-1} = X + (1 - b(0))^{-1} (S^* b \otimes k_0^b).$$

(III-9) Multipliers. *If φ is a multiplier of $\mathcal{H}(b)$, then the operator $V_b^{-1} M_\varphi^* V_b$ coincides on functions in the disk algebra with the operator $T_{\overline{\varphi}}$.*

By the disk algebra is meant, as usual, the space of functions that are continuous in $\overline{D}$ and holomorphic in D. If φ is a multiplier of $\mathcal{H}(b)$ then, because $V_b^{-1} k_w^b = (1 - \overline{b(w)}) k_w$, the function k_w is an eigenvector of $V_b^{-1} M_\varphi^* V_b$ with eigenvalue $\overline{\varphi(w)}$. Hence $V_b^{-1} M_\varphi^* V_b$ and $T_{\overline{\varphi}}$ coincide on the linear span of the functions k_w. The desired conclusion now follows because the linear span of the functions k_w is uniformly dense in the disk algebra.

(III-10) A Multiplier Criterion. *For the function φ in H^∞ to be a multiplier of $\mathcal{H}(b)$, it is necessary and sufficient that the restriction of $T_{\overline{\varphi}}$ to the disk algebra be bounded in the norm of $L^2(\mu)$.*

In fact, the necessity is given by (III-9). To obtain the sufficiency one notes that, if $T_{\overline{\varphi}}$ has the required boundedness property, then V_b transforms it to a bounded operator on $\mathcal{H}(b)$ having each kernel function k_w^b as an eigenvector, the corresponding eigenvalue being $\overline{\varphi(w)}$. The sufficiency thus follows from (II-10).

(III-11) Comparison of Measures. *Let u be a nonconstant inner function, and let ν be the measure on ∂D whose Poisson integral is the real part of $\dfrac{1+u}{1-u}$. The following conditions are equivalent:*

(i) ν is absolutely continuous with respect to μ and $\dfrac{d\nu}{d\mu}$ is in $L^2(\mu)$;

(ii) the function $\left(\dfrac{1-b}{1-u}\right)k_0^u$ is in $\mathcal{H}(b)$.

To establish this, suppose first that condition (i) holds. Then the function $V_b\left(\dfrac{d\nu}{d\mu}\right)$ is in $\mathcal{H}(b)$. But

$$V_b\left(\frac{d\nu}{d\mu}\right) = (1-b)K_\mu\left(\frac{d\nu}{d\mu}\right) = (1-b)K_\nu(1)$$
$$= \left(\frac{1-b}{1-u}\right)V_\nu(1) = (1-\overline{u(0)})^{-1}\left(\frac{1-b}{1-u}\right)k_0^u,$$

and so condition (ii) holds.

Suppose, conversely, that condition (ii) holds. Then there is a function q in $L^2(\mu)$ such that $\left(\dfrac{1-b}{1-u}\right)k_0^u = V_b q$, in other words, $\dfrac{1-\overline{u(0)}u}{1-u} = K_\mu q$. Thus, for z in D,

$$\frac{1-\overline{u(0)}u(z)}{1-u(z)} = \int_{\partial D}\frac{q(e^{i\theta})}{1-e^{-i\theta}z}d\mu(e^{i\theta})$$
$$= \frac{1}{2}\int_{\partial D}\left(\frac{e^{i\theta}+z}{e^{i\theta}-z}+1\right)q(e^{i\theta})d\mu(e^{i\theta})$$
$$= \frac{1}{2}\left[\int_{\partial D}\left(\frac{e^{i\theta}+z}{e^{i\theta}-z}\right)q(e^{i\theta})d\mu(e^{i\theta}) + \frac{1-|u(0)|^2}{1-u(0)}\right].$$

In the preceding string of equalities, the left side can be rewritten as $\overline{u(0)} + \dfrac{1-\overline{u(0)}}{1-u(z)}$. We thus have

$$\frac{1+u(z)}{1-u(z)} = \frac{2}{1-u(z)} - 1$$
$$= (1-\overline{u(0)})^{-1}\int_{\partial D}\left(\frac{e^{i\theta}+z}{e^{i\theta}-z}\right)q(e^{i\theta})d\mu(e^{i\theta})$$
$$+ \frac{1-|u(0)|^2}{|1-u(0)|^2} - \frac{2\overline{u(0)}}{1-\overline{u(0)}} - 1.$$

The last three terms on the right side sum to $i \operatorname{Im} \left(\dfrac{1 + u(0)}{1 - u(0)} \right)$. It follows, therefore, that the measures $(1 - \overline{u(0)})^{-1} q\mu$ and ν have the same Herglotz integral. Since ν is singular, the F. and M. Riesz theorem implies that it must coincide with the singular component of $(1 - \overline{u(0)})^{-1} q\mu$, and thus (i) holds.

(III-12) A Consequence. Letting z_0 be a point of ∂D and applying (III-11) to the inner function $u(z) = z/z_0$, we draw the following conclusion: The measure μ has an atom at the point z_0 if and only if the function $\dfrac{b(z) - 1}{z - z_0}$ lies in $\mathcal{H}(b)$.

Notes

(NIII-1) The Cauchy integral representation (III-2) for $\mathcal{H}(\bar{b})$ is from the paper [44] of Lotto and the author.

(NIII-2) For the case where b is an inner function, which happens if and only if the measure μ is singular, the Cauchy integral representation (III-7) for $\mathcal{H}(b)$ was discovered by D. N. Clark [18]. The representation of Clark was extended to vector-valued de Branges–Rovnyak spaces by Ball in his dissertation [7]; that result also appears in Ball's paper with Lubin [10]. The formula in (III-6) for $\langle k_z, k_w \rangle_\mu$, which lies at the heart of the representation of $\mathcal{H}(b)$, can be found, also in a vector-valued context, in one of the papers of Alpay and Dym [4, Lemma 6.4].

(NIII-3) A. G. Poltoratskii [S8] has recently proved that, in the case where the measure μ is singular (i.e., the case where b is an inner function), one obtains the inverse of the transformation V_b by taking boundary values. To be more precise, assume μ is singular, let q be a function in $L^2(\mu)$, let $h = V_b q$, and for $0 < r < 1$ define the function h_r on ∂D by $h_r(e^{i\theta}) = h(re^{i\theta})$. Then $h_r \to q$ in the norm of $L^2(\mu)$ as $r \to 1$, and, at almost every point of ∂D relative to μ, the function h has a nontangential limit agreeing with the value of the function q. More generally, as Poltoratskii shows, if μ is not singular, then the limiting behavior just described still takes place relative to the singular component of μ. It is expected that Poltoratskii's results will be important in the further development of the theory.

(NIII-4) Cauchy integrals in the unit disk (often called integrals of Cauchy–Stieltjes type) have been studied in depth by several people beginning with V. P. Havin [29]. Further references can be found in the expository article [17] of J. A. Cima and T. H. MacGregor. The connection with $\mathcal{H}(b)$ given by (III-7) should be useful in the further study of Cauchy integrals. It has been used by Lotto and the author [44], for example, to give a simple proof of a theorem of S. A. Vinogradov [67].

(NIII-5) For the case where b is an inner function, (III-11) appears (in a slightly different form) in the author's paper [63]. The result there is based on an observation of D. Hitt. Later on, in (IV-8) and (V-9), the criterion in (III-11) will be elaborated.

(NIII-6) B. M. Davis and J. E. McCarthy [20] have exploited the criterion in (III-10) to study multipliers of $\mathcal{H}(b)$.

CHAPTER IV

NONEXTREME POINTS

The study of $\mathcal{H}(b)$ frequently bifurcates into two cases, the case where the function $\log(1 - |b|^2)$ is integrable on ∂D and the case where it is not. It is known that $\log(1 - |b|^2)$ is integrable if and only if b fails to be an extreme point of the unit ball of H^∞ (a reference is given in (NIV-1)); when the latter happens we shall say simply that b is nonextreme, and in the contrary case we shall say that b is extreme. This chapter concerns the case where b is nonextreme.

When b is nonextreme, the space $\mathcal{H}(\overline{b})$ is the range of a certain conjugate-analytic Toeplitz operator, from which it follows easily that the polynomials are contained in and are dense in $\mathcal{H}(\overline{b})$. The polynomials are also dense in $\mathcal{H}(b)$ because, as will be shown, $\mathcal{H}(\overline{b})$ is dense in $\mathcal{H}(b)$ (when b is nonextreme). Other properties characteristic of the case where b is nonextreme are: $\mathcal{H}(b)$ contains b, it is invariant under the (forward) shift operator, and every function holomorphic on $\overline{D}$ is a multiplier.

The absolutely continuous component of the measure μ has density $\dfrac{1 - |b|^2}{|1 - b|^2}$ on ∂D (since μ is by definition the measure whose Poisson integral equals the preceding function in D). The H^2 space of the weight $\dfrac{1 - |b|^2}{|1 - b|^2}$ can thus be regarded as a subspace of $H^2(\mu)$, a subspace that equals $H^2(\mu)$ if and only if μ is absolutely continuous. If b is nonextreme then, as we shall see, the weight $\dfrac{1 - |b|^2}{|1 - b|^2}$ equals the square of the modulus of an outer function in H^2. That provides a natural isometry of H^2 onto the H^2 space of the preceding weight which, when followed by the isometry V_b from Chapter III, gives an isometry of H^2 into $\mathcal{H}(b)$. The last isometry is surjective if and only if μ is absolutely continuous.

If λ is a complex number of modulus 1, then the spaces $\mathcal{H}(b)$ and $\mathcal{H}(\overline{\lambda}b)$ are identical. For each such λ one gets a different Cauchy integral representation of $\mathcal{H}(b)$. If b is nonextreme, then for each λ one gets by the recipe described in

23

the preceding paragraph a different isometry of H^2 into $\mathcal{H}(b)$. If one follows one of these isometries by the adjoint of another, one obtains a contraction of H^2 into itself. Below we shall obtain an explicit expression in terms of Toeplitz operators for such a contraction. An interesting consequence is that certain unbounded Toeplitz operators have bounded products. The latter circumstance will be used in deriving a divisibility property associated with the case where μ is not absolutely continuous and related to a question about rigid functions to be discussed in Chapter X.

Also in this chapter, the Sz.-Nagy-Foias model for the restricted backward shift in $\mathcal{H}(b)$ is worked out for the case where b is nonextreme, and the absolute continuity criterion from the last chapter is adapted to that case.

(IV-1) The Function a. When b is nonextreme, we let a denote the outer function that has modulus $(1 - |b|^2)^{1/2}$ on ∂D and that is positive at the origin. Then $T_{\bar{a}}T_a = 1 - T_{\bar{b}}T_b$, which implies, in virtue of (I-5)(ii), that $\mathcal{H}(\bar{b}) = \mathcal{M}(\bar{a})$. From (I-5)(i) and the inequality $T_a T_{\bar{a}} \leq T_{\bar{a}} T_a$ one sees that $\mathcal{M}(a)$ is contained contractively in $\mathcal{M}(\bar{a})$ and hence also in $\mathcal{H}(b)$.

If b is nonextreme and h is a function in H^2 then, by (II-4), h belongs to $\mathcal{H}(b)$ if and only if $T_{\bar{b}}h$ is in $\mathcal{M}(\bar{a})$; when that happens there is a unique function h^+ in H^2 such that $T_{\bar{b}}h = T_{\bar{a}}h^+$. (Uniqueness holds because $T_{\bar{a}}$ has a trivial kernel, a being an outer function.) If h_1 and h_2 are two functions in $\mathcal{H}(b)$, then

$$\langle h_1, h_2 \rangle_b = \langle h_1, h_2 \rangle + \langle h_1^+, h_2^+ \rangle.$$

For example,

$$T_{\bar{b}}S^*b = S^*P_+(|b|^2) = S^*P_+(1 - |a|^2)$$
$$= -T_{\bar{a}}S^*a,$$

so that $(S^*b)^+ = -S^*a$, and

$$\|S^*b\|_b^2 = \|S^*b\|_2^2 + \|S^*a\|_2^2$$
$$= \|b\|_2^2 - |b(0)|^2 + \|a\|_2^2 - |a(0)|^2$$
$$= 1 - |b(0)|^2 - |a(0)|^2.$$

Note that if h is in $\mathcal{H}(b)$ and φ is in H^∞, then

$$T_{\bar{b}}T_{\bar{\varphi}}h = T_{\bar{\varphi}}T_{\bar{b}}h = T_{\bar{\varphi}}T_{\bar{a}}h^+ = T_{\bar{a}}T_{\bar{\varphi}}h^+,$$

showing that $(T_{\bar{\varphi}}h)^+ = T_{\bar{\varphi}}h^+$.

(IV-2) Polynomials. *If b is nonextreme, then the polynomials belong to $\mathcal{M}(\overline{a})$ and are dense in $\mathcal{M}(\overline{a})$.*

Since the image under $T_{\overline{a}}$ of a polynomial is a polynomial of the same degree, and the polynomials are dense in H^2, the proposition is obvious.

(IV-3) Density. *If b is nonextreme, then $\mathcal{M}(\overline{a})$ is dense in $\mathcal{H}(b)$. Hence the polynomials are dense in $\mathcal{H}(b)$.*

Suppose the function h in $\mathcal{H}(b)$ is orthogonal to $\mathcal{M}(\overline{a})$ (relative to the inner product in $\mathcal{H}(b)$). Then h is orthogonal to $T_{\overline{a}}S^{*n}h$ for every nonnegative integer n. Because $(T_{\overline{a}}S^{*n}h)^+ = T_{\overline{a}}S^{*n}h^+$ (as noted in (IV-1)), we have, for $n = 0, 1, \ldots,$

$$\begin{aligned}
0 &= \langle h, T_{\overline{a}}S^{*n}h\rangle_b \\
&= \langle h, T_{\overline{a}}S^{*n}h\rangle + \langle h^+, T_{\overline{a}}S^{*n}h^+\rangle \\
&= \frac{1}{2\pi}\int_{\partial D} a(e^{i\theta})(|h(e^{i\theta})|^2 + |h^+(e^{i\theta})|^2)e^{in\theta}d\theta.
\end{aligned}$$

It follows that the function $a(|h|^2 + |h^+|^2)$ belongs to H_0^1. Since a is an outer function, the function $|h|^2 + |h^+|^2$ must then also belong to H_0^1. Since the only real-valued function in H_0^1 is the zero function, it follows that $h = 0$, as desired.

(IV-4) Inclusion of b. *If b is nonextreme, then b belongs to $\mathcal{H}(b)$, and $\|b\|_b^2 = |a(0)|^{-2} - 1$.*

To prove this we note that

$$\begin{aligned}
T_{\overline{b}}b &= P_+(|b|^2) = P_+(1 - |a|^2) \\
&= T_{\overline{a}}(1/\overline{a(0)} - a).
\end{aligned}$$

It follows that b is in $\mathcal{H}(b)$ and $b^+ = 1/\overline{a(0)} - a$. Thus

$$\begin{aligned}
\|b\|_b^2 &= \|b\|_2^2 + \|1/\overline{a(0)} - a\|_2^2 \\
&= \|b\|_2^2 + \|a - a(0)\|^2 + |1/\overline{a(0)} - a(0)|^2 \\
&= \|b\|_2^2 + \|a\|_2^2 - |a(0)|^2 + |a(0)|^{-2} + |a(0)|^2 - 2 \\
&= |a(0)|^{-2} - 1.
\end{aligned}$$

(IV-5) Shift invariance. *If b is nonextreme then the space $\mathcal{H}(b)$ is invariant under the unilateral shift, S. The spectrum of the restriction of S to $\mathcal{H}(b)$ is $\overline{D}$.*

The S-invariance of $\mathcal{H}(b)$ follows from the formula

$$X^*h = Sh - \langle h, S^*b\rangle_b b \qquad (h \in \mathcal{H}(b)),$$

obtained in (II-9), plus the inclusion of b in $\mathcal{H}(b)$, just established. The formula shows also that $S|\mathcal{H}(b)$ is a rank-one perturbation of a contraction. Therefore, by Fredholm theory, any spectral points of $S|\mathcal{H}(b)$ outside $\overline{D}$ must be eigenvectors. But S has no eigenvectors, so the spectrum of $S|\mathcal{H}(b)$ is contained in $\overline{D}$. The opposite inclusion is obvious.

(IV-6) Multipliers. *If b is nonextreme, then all functions holomorphic on $\overline{D}$ are multipliers of $\mathcal{H}(b)$ and of $\mathcal{M}(\overline{a})$. In particular, such functions belong to $\mathcal{M}(\overline{a})$.*

If φ is holomorphic on $\overline{D}$ then, since the spectrum of $S|\mathcal{H}(b)$ is $\overline{D}$, the operator $\varphi(S|\mathcal{H}(b))$ is defined by the Riesz–Dunford functional calculus, and it clearly coincides with the operator of multiplication by φ. This establishes the proposition for $\mathcal{H}(b)$, and the case of $\mathcal{M}(\overline{a})$ follows because every multiplier of $\mathcal{H}(b)$ is one of $\mathcal{M}(\overline{a})$, as noted in (II-10).

(IV-7) Sz.–Nagy–Foias model for X. Let b be nonextreme. According to (IV-1) the map $h \mapsto h \oplus h^+$ is an isometry of $\mathcal{H}(b)$ onto a certain subspace of $H^2 \oplus H^2$. What is this subspace? Since it consists of all vectors $h_1 \oplus h_2$ in $H^2 \oplus H^2$ such that $T_{\overline{b}}h_1 = T_{\overline{a}}h_2$, it is the kernel of the operator $[T_{\overline{b}} \ \ -T_{\overline{a}}]$ from $H^2 \oplus H^2$ to H^2, in other words, it is the orthogonal complement of the range of the operator

$$B = \begin{bmatrix} T_b \\ -T_a \end{bmatrix}$$

from H^2 to $H^2 \oplus H^2$. Because $|b|^2 + |a|^2 = 1$ on ∂D the operator B is an isometry, so the subspace in question is $\mathcal{H}(B)$. Letting Q denote the projection in $H^2 \oplus H^2$ onto the first coordinate space, we thus see that $Q|\mathcal{H}(B)$ is an isometry of $\mathcal{H}(B)$ onto $\mathcal{H}(b)$. As this isometry intertwines $(S^* \oplus S^*) | \mathcal{H}(B)$ with X, the former operator is the Sz.–Nagy–Foias model of X.

The preceding discussion shows that $\mathcal{H}(b) = \mathcal{M}(Q(1-BB^*))$, an equality that is easily seen directly. In fact, $1 - BB^*$ is the two-by-two operator matrix
$$\begin{bmatrix} 1 - T_b T_{\bar{b}} & T_b T_{\bar{a}} \\ T_a T_{\bar{b}} & 1 - T_a T_{\bar{a}} \end{bmatrix},$$
whose upper-left entry is $1 - T_b T_{\bar{b}}$, meaning that $Q(1 - BB^*)Q = 1 - T_b T_{\bar{b}}$. The lower-right entry in the matrix is $1 - T_a T_{\bar{a}}$, implying that $\mathcal{H}(a) = \mathcal{M}((1 - Q)(1 - BB^*))$, in other words, the operator $(1 - Q)|\mathcal{H}(B)$ is a partial isometry of $\mathcal{H}(B)$ onto $\mathcal{H}(a)$, a partial isometry whose kernel is easily seen to equal $\ker T_{\bar{b}}$. Differently put, the map $h \mapsto h^+$ is a partial isometry of $\mathcal{H}(b)$ onto $\mathcal{H}(a)$ with kernel equal to $\ker T_{\bar{b}}$.

(IV-8) Comparison of measures. *Let b be nonextreme, let u be a nonconstant inner function, and let ν be the measure on ∂D whose Poisson integral is the real part of $\dfrac{1+u}{1-u}$. The following conditions are equivalent:*

(i) ν is absolutely continuous with respect to μ and $\dfrac{d\nu}{d\mu}$ is in $L^2(\mu)$;

(ii) the functions $\dfrac{1-b}{1-u}$ and $\dfrac{a}{1-u}$ are in H^2.

By (III-11), condition (i) holds if and only if the function $\left(\dfrac{1-b}{1-u}\right) k_0^u$ is in $\mathcal{H}(b)$. But that happens if and only if $\dfrac{1-b}{1-u}$ is in $\mathcal{H}(b)$, because

$$\left(\frac{1-b}{1-u}\right) k_0^u = (1 - \overline{u(0)}) \left(\frac{1-b}{1-u}\right) + \overline{u(0)}(1-b),$$

and $1 - b$ belongs to $\mathcal{H}(b)$. It will thus suffice to show that condition (ii) holds if and only if $\dfrac{1-b}{1-u}$ is in $\mathcal{H}(b)$.

Assume condition (ii) holds. Then

$$T_{\bar{b}}\left(\frac{1-b}{1-u}\right) = P_+\left(\frac{1-|b|^2}{1-u}\right) + P_+\left(\frac{\bar{b}-1}{1-u}\right)$$
$$= P_+\left(\frac{|a|^2}{1-u}\right) + P_+\left(\frac{\bar{u}(\bar{b}-1)}{\bar{u}-1}\right).$$

The first term on the right equals $T_{\bar{a}}\left(\dfrac{a}{1-u}\right)$ and so is in $\mathcal{M}(\bar{a})$. The second term on the right is a constant function, since it is the projection of a function in $\overline{H}^2$; it is thus also in $\mathcal{M}(\overline{a})$. Since $T_{\overline{b}}\left(\dfrac{1-b}{1-u}\right)$ is in $\mathcal{M}(\overline{a})$, the function $\dfrac{1-b}{1-u}$ is in $\mathcal{H}(b)$, as desired.

Assume, conversely, that $\dfrac{1-b}{1-u}$ is in $\mathcal{H}(b)$. Then there is a function f in H^2 such that $T_{\overline{a}}f = T_{\overline{b}}\left(\dfrac{1-b}{1-u}\right)$. As above we have

$$T_{\overline{b}}\left(\frac{1-b}{1-u}\right) = P_+\left(\frac{|a|^2}{1-u}\right) + c,$$

where c is a constant. Letting $g = f - c/\overline{a(0)}$, we thus have

$$T_{\overline{a}}g = P_+\left(\frac{|a|^2}{1-u}\right),$$

in other words,

$$P_+\left(\frac{|a|^2}{1-u} - \overline{a}g\right) = 0.$$

The function $\overline{a}\left(\dfrac{a}{1-u} - g\right)$ is thus in $\overline{H}_0^2$.

We now need the observation that the function $\dfrac{a}{1-b}$ lies in H^2. In fact, this function is outer, and on ∂D the square of its modulus equals $(1 - |b|^2)/|1-b|^2$, which is the boundary function of $\operatorname{Re}\dfrac{1+b}{1-b}$ and thus is the normalized Radon–Nikodym derivative of the absolutely continuous component of the measure μ. In particular, $|a|^2/|1-b|^2$ is in L^1 on ∂D, implying that $\left(\dfrac{a}{1-b}\right)^2$ is in H^1 and hence that $\dfrac{a}{1-b}$ is in H^2.

From the preceding observation it follows that the function $\dfrac{a}{1-u}$ is in H^1, for it is the product of the H^2 functions $\dfrac{1-b}{1-u}$ and $\dfrac{a}{1-b}$. Thus, the function $\dfrac{a}{1-u} - g$ is in H^1. But it is shown above that the function $a\left(\dfrac{\overline{a}}{1-\overline{u}} - \overline{g}\right)$ is in H_0^2. Since $\dfrac{\overline{a}}{1-\overline{u}} - \overline{g}$ is in L^1 and a is outer, we can conclude that $\dfrac{\overline{a}}{1-\overline{u}} - \overline{g}$ is in H_0^1, in other words, $\dfrac{a}{1-u} - g$ is in $\overline{H}_0^1$. Since $H^1 \cap \overline{H}_0^1$ contains only the zero function, we have $\dfrac{a}{1-u} = g$, showing that $\dfrac{a}{1-u}$ is in H^2, the desired conclusion.

(IV-9) The functions F and F_λ. Assume b is nonextreme. The function $\dfrac{a}{1-b}$ that turned up in the preceding proof will be denoted henceforth by F. As noted above, it belongs to H^2, and the square of its H^2 norm is at most the norm of μ, which equals $(1-|b(0)|^2)/|1-b(0)|^2$ (the value of $\operatorname{Re}\dfrac{1+b}{1-b}$ at the origin). The equality $\|F\|_2^2 = (1-|b(0)|^2)/|1-b(0)|^2$ holds if and only if the measure μ is absolutely continuous.

If λ is a point of ∂D and we replace the function b by the function $\overline{\lambda}b$, we do not change the space $\mathcal{H}(b)$, yet we replace the measure μ by a new measure, which will be called μ_λ. (In other words, μ_λ is the measure on ∂D whose Poisson integral is the real part of $\dfrac{\lambda+b}{\lambda-b}$. Its definition obviously does not depend upon the assumption that b is nonextreme.) The corresponding function $\dfrac{a}{1-\overline{\lambda}b}$ will be denoted by F_λ. The normalized Radon–Nikodym derivative of the absolutely continuous component of μ_λ is thus $|F_\lambda|^2$.

(IV-10) The measure μ_λ is usually absolutely continuous. *Assume b is nonextreme (or, more generally, that $|b|<1$ almost everywhere on ∂D). Then the measure μ_λ is absolutely continuous for almost every λ in ∂D.*

The norm of μ_λ is $\dfrac{1-|b(0)|^2}{|\lambda-b(0)|^2}$, and the norm of its absolutely continuous component is the L^1 norm of the function $\dfrac{1-|b(e^{i\theta})|^2}{|\lambda-b(e^{i\theta})|^2}$. Hence, to prove the proposition, it will be enough to show that

$$\int_{\partial D} \frac{1-|b(0)|^2}{|e^{it}-b(0)|^2}\frac{dt}{2\pi} = \int_{\partial D}\int_{\partial D} \frac{1-|b(e^{i\theta})|^2}{|e^{it}-b(e^{i\theta})|^2}\frac{d\theta}{2\pi}\frac{dt}{2\pi}.$$

The integrand in the integral on the left side is the Poisson kernel for the point $b(0)$; the integral on the left is therefore 1. For fixed θ, the integrand in the integral on the right side is the Poisson kernel for the point $b(e^{i\theta})$, provided $|b(e^{i\theta})|<1$, which is the case for almost every θ. After one changes the order of integration on the right side, therefore, the inside integrals almost all have the value 1, so the integral on the right is also 1, as desired.

(IV-11) Observations, and an example. It is known that the Poisson integral of a positive measure on ∂D tends radially to $+\infty$ almost everywhere with respect to the singular component of the measure. (References are noted in (NIV-8).) Hence, for λ in ∂D, the function b has the radial limit λ almost everywhere with respect to the singular component of μ_λ. The singular components of the various measures μ_λ are thus carried by mutually disjoint sets and so are mutually singular. If b happens to have no radial limits of unit modulus, then every measure μ_λ is absolutely continuous.

The function $b(z) = \dfrac{1+z}{2}$ provides a simple illustration. The corresponding function a is easily seen to be $\dfrac{1-z}{2}$. The function b has the radial limit 1 at the point 1 and no other radial limit of unit modulus. Hence, in view of the remarks above, the corresponding measures μ_λ are absolutely continuous except possibly for μ_1, whose singular component is at most an atom at the point 1. That the preceding singular component is in fact nonzero follows from the criterion (III-12). (In our example the function $\dfrac{1-b(z)}{1-z}$ is the constant function $1/2$ and so belongs to $\mathcal{H}(b)$.) The preceding conclusions are of course easily verified directly. In particular, the function F_1 in this example turns out to be the constant function 1, so its norm is 1, while $\|\mu_1\| = (1 - |b(0)|^2)/|1 - b(0)|^2 = 3$.

(IV-12) Toeplitz operators with L^2 symbols. As we are about to run into possibly unbounded Toeplitz operators, a few remarks about them are in order. For φ a function in L^2, we define the operator T_φ on H^2 by $T_\varphi f = K(\varphi f)|D$. This is equivalent to the standard definition when φ is bounded. If φ is unbounded, then T_φ is not a bounded operator on H^2, but it is a continuous operator of H^2 into $H(D)$, the space of holomorphic functions on D with the topology of locally uniform convergence. If φ is in L^2 and ψ is in H^2, then the product $T_\psi T_\varphi$ makes obvious sense (namely, $T_\psi T_\varphi h$ should be interpreted as $\psi T_\varphi h$).

(IV-13) From H^2 to $\mathcal{H}(b)$. Assume b is nonextreme. The function $|F|^2$ is the normalized Radon–Nikodym derivative of the absolutely continuous component, μ_a, of the measure μ. The map $f \mapsto F^{-1}f$ thus defines an isometry of H^2 onto $H^2(\mu_a)$. The space $H^2(\mu)$ is the direct sum of $H^2(\mu_a)$ and the L^2 space of the singular component of μ (as one can deduce from the F. and M. Riesz theorem). The map $f \mapsto F^{-1}f$ can thus be regarded as an isometry of H^2 into $H^2(\mu)$, and if we follow it by the map V_b we get an isometry of H^2 into $\mathcal{H}(b)$, an isometry whose range is all of $\mathcal{H}(b)$ if and only if μ is absolutely continuous. The image of the H^2 function f under the latter isometry is $(1-b)K(F^{-1}f|F|^2)|D$, which is the same as $T_{1-b}T_{\overline{F}}f$. Thus, the operator $T_{1-b}T_{\overline{F}}$ is an isometry of H^2 into $\mathcal{H}(b)$; its range is all of $\mathcal{H}(b)$ if and only if μ is absolutely continuous. In particular, $T_{1-b}T_{\overline{F}}$ is a bounded operator on H^2 of norm at most 1.

If μ is absolutely continuous we thus have $\mathcal{H}(b) = \mathcal{M}(T_{1-b}T_{\overline{F}})$. It then follows by (I-5)(ii) that $(T_{1-b}T_{\overline{F}})(T_{1-b}T_{\overline{F}})^* = 1 - T_b T_{\overline{b}}$, in other words, $(T_{1-b}T_{\overline{F}})(T_F T_{1-\overline{b}}) = 1 - T_b T_{\overline{b}}$ (since $T_F T_{1-\overline{b}}$ is easily seen to be the adjoint of $T_{1-b}T_{\overline{F}}$).

(IV-14) From H^2 to $\mathcal{H}(a)$. Assume b is nonextreme. If f is a function in H^2 then, by (IV-13), the function $T_{1-b}T_{\overline{F}}f$ is in $\mathcal{H}(b)$, and so the function $T_{\overline{b}}(T_{1-b}T_{\overline{F}})f$ is in $\mathcal{M}(\overline{a})$. Formally we have

$$\begin{aligned}T_{\overline{b}}T_{1-b}T_{\overline{F}} &= (T_{\overline{b}} - T_{|b|^2})T_{\overline{F}} \\ &= T_{1-|b|^2}T_{\overline{F}} - T_{1-\overline{b}}T_{\overline{F}} \\ &= T_{\overline{a}}T_a T_{\overline{F}} - T_{\overline{a}} \\ &= -T_{\overline{a}}(1 - T_a T_{\overline{F}}).\end{aligned}$$

This suggests that, if f is in H^2 and $h = T_{1-b}T_{\overline{F}}f$, then $-(1-T_a T_{\overline{F}})f$ should be h^+, and thus (in accord with the observation at the end of (IV-7)) the operator $1 - T_a T_{\overline{F}}$ should map H^2 into $\mathcal{H}(a)$.

The reasoning can be made rigorous. Namely, if in the formal manipulations above we apply each operator that appears to a polynomial p, then the resulting equalities are all easily seen to be correct. We thus have

$$T_{\overline{b}}(T_{1-b}T_{\overline{F}})p = -T_{\overline{a}}(1 - T_a T_{\overline{F}})p$$

for every polynomial p. Now let f be any function in H^2 and let $(p_n)_1^\infty$ be a sequence of polynomials converging to f in L^2 norm. Let $h = T_{1-b}T_{\overline{F}}f$ and $h_n = T_{1-b}T_{\overline{F}}p_n$. Then $h_n \to h$ in $\mathcal{H}(b)$ norm, so $h_n^+ \to h^+$ in $\mathcal{H}(a)$ norm (by the observation at the end of (IV-7)). But $h_n^+ = -(1-T_a T_{\overline{F}})p_n$ by the equality above applied to the polynomial $p = p_n$, and $(1 - T_a T_{\overline{F}})p_n \to (1 - T_a T_{\overline{F}})f$ locally uniformly in D. We can conclude that $(1 - T_a T_{\overline{F}})f = -h^+$, so the operator $1 - T_a T_{\overline{F}}$ maps H^2 into $\mathcal{H}(a)$. In fact, the preceding operator is a contraction of H^2 into $\mathcal{H}(a)$, because the map $h \mapsto h^+$ is a contraction of $\mathcal{H}(b)$ onto $\mathcal{H}(a)$. In particular, the operator $T_a T_{\overline{F}}$ is a bounded operator on H^2, of norm at most 2.

If μ is absolutely continuous, the operator $T_{1-b}T_{\overline{F}}$ sends H^2 isometrically onto $\mathcal{H}(b)$, and the reasoning above shows that the operator $1 - T_a T_{\overline{F}}$ sends H^2 coisometrically onto $\mathcal{H}(a)$, in other words, $\mathcal{H}(a) = \mathcal{M}(1 - T_a T_{\overline{F}})$.

(IV-15) Two formulas. *If b is nonextreme then, for h in $\mathcal{H}(b)$ and w in D,*

$$\langle h, k_w \rangle_b = h(w) + \frac{b(w)}{a(w)} h^+(w)$$

$$\langle h, bk_w \rangle_b = \frac{h^+(w)}{a(w)}.$$

In fact, since $T_{\bar{b}} k_w = \overline{b(w)} k_w$ and $T_{\bar{a}} k_w = \overline{a(w)} k_w$, we have $k_w^+ = \overline{\frac{b(w)}{a(w)}} k_w$. Therefore

$$\langle h, k_w \rangle_b = \langle h, k_w \rangle + \langle h^+, k_w^+ \rangle$$
$$= h(w) + \frac{b(w)}{a(w)} h^+(w),$$

which is the first formula. The second formula follows from the first formula in conjunction with the equality $k_w^b = k_w - \overline{b(w)} bk_w$. Namely, we have

$$b(w) \langle h, bk_w \rangle_b = \langle h, k_w \rangle_b - \langle h, k_w^b \rangle_b$$
$$= h(w) + \frac{b(w)}{a(w)} h^+(w) - h(w)$$
$$= \frac{b(w)}{a(w)} h^+(w),$$

which implies the second formula if $b(w) \neq 0$. At the zeros of b the result follows by continuity.

Three special cases of the formulas are needed below: the first formula when $h = k_z$, and the second formula when $h = k_z$ and when $h = bk_z$. The results are as follows:

$$\langle k_z, k_w \rangle_b = \left(1 + \frac{\overline{b(z)} b(w)}{\overline{a(z)} a(w)} \right) k_z(w)$$

$$\langle k_z, bk_w \rangle_b = \frac{\overline{b(z)}}{\overline{a(z)} a(w)} k_z(w)$$

$$\langle bk_z, bk_w \rangle_b = \left(\frac{1}{\overline{a(z)} a(w)} - 1 \right) k_z(w).$$

One obtains the first two of these by routine substitution. To obtain the third one needs the equality

$$(bk_z)^+ = \left(\frac{1}{\overline{a(z)}} - a \right) k_z,$$

whose derivation is straightforward.

(IV-16) From H^2 to $\mathcal{H}(b)$ and back. Assume b is nonextreme. For each λ in ∂D we let W_λ denote the operator $T_{1-\overline{\lambda}b}T_{\overline{F}_\lambda}$, regarded as an operator from H^2 into $\mathcal{H}(b)$; it is an isometry, as shown in (IV-13). Thus W_λ^* is a coisometry of $\mathcal{H}(b)$ onto H^2.

Let η and λ be two points of ∂D. We shall investigate the operator $W_\lambda^* W_\eta$, which is a contraction of H^2 into itself. (It is in fact a unitary operator if μ_λ and μ_η are both absolutely continuous, which is the case for almost every pair λ, η.)

Let z and w be points of D. We have

$$\langle W_\lambda^* W_\eta k_z, k_w \rangle = \langle W_\eta k_z, W_\lambda k_w \rangle_b$$
$$= \langle T_{1-\overline{\eta}b} T_{\overline{F}_\eta} k_z, T_{1-\overline{\lambda}b} T_{\overline{F}_\lambda} k_w \rangle_b$$
$$= \overline{F_\eta(z)} F_\lambda(w) \langle (1-\overline{\eta}b)k_z, (1-\overline{\lambda}b)k_w \rangle_b.$$

We use the formulas at the end of (IV-15) to evaluate the inner product on the right side. The calculation is straightforward:

$$\langle (1-\overline{\eta}b)k_z, (1-\overline{\lambda}b)k_w \rangle_b = \langle k_z, k_w \rangle_b - \overline{\eta}\langle bk_z, k_w \rangle_b$$
$$- \lambda \langle k_z, bk_w \rangle_b + \overline{\eta}\lambda \langle bk_z, bk_w \rangle_b$$
$$= \left(1 + \frac{\overline{b(z)}b(w)}{\overline{a(z)}a(w)}\right) k_z(w) - \overline{\eta}\left(\frac{b(w)}{\overline{a(z)}a(w)}\right) k_z(w)$$
$$- \lambda \left(\frac{\overline{b(z)}}{\overline{a(z)}a(w)}\right) k_z(w)$$
$$+ \overline{\eta}\lambda \left(\frac{1}{\overline{a(z)}a(w)} - 1\right) k_z(w)$$
$$= \left[1 - \overline{\eta}\lambda + \frac{\overline{\eta}\lambda(1-\eta\overline{b(z)})(1-\overline{\lambda}b(w))}{\overline{a(z)}a(w)}\right] k_z(w)$$
$$= [1 - \overline{\eta}\lambda + \overline{\eta}\lambda \overline{F_\eta(z)}^{-1} F_\lambda(w)^{-1}] k_z(w).$$

We thus have

$$\langle W_\lambda^* W_\eta k_z, k_w \rangle = (1-\overline{\eta}\lambda)\overline{F_\eta(z)} F_\lambda(w) k_z(w) + \overline{\eta}\lambda k_z(w)$$
$$= (1-\overline{\eta}\lambda)\langle T_{\overline{F}_\eta} k_z, T_{\overline{F}_\lambda} k_w \rangle + \overline{\eta}\lambda \langle k_z, k_w \rangle$$
$$= \langle [(1-\lambda\overline{\eta})T_{F_\lambda} T_{\overline{F}_\eta} + \lambda\overline{\eta}]k_z, k_w \rangle,$$

showing that the two operators $W_\lambda^* W_\eta$ and $(1-\lambda\bar\eta)T_{F_\lambda}T_{\overline{F}_\eta} + \lambda\bar\eta$ agree on all the kernel functions k_z. Since those kernel functions span H^2 and since both operators are continuous as maps from H^2 to $H(D)$, they must be equal. Thus $T_{F_\lambda}T_{\overline{F}_\eta}$ is in fact a bounded operator on H^2 if $\lambda \neq \eta$, with norm at most $2/|\lambda - \eta|$.

(IV-17) Singular measures and divisibility. *Assume b is nonextreme. Let u be a nonconstant inner function, and let ν be the measure on ∂D whose Poisson integral is the real part of $\dfrac{1+u}{1-u}$. If ν is absolutely continuous with respect to μ and $d\nu/d\mu$ is in $L^2(\mu)$, then the function $F_\lambda/(1-u)$ is in H^2 for all λ in $\partial D\setminus\{1\}$.*

In fact, if ν satisfies the given conditions, then the function $h = V_b(d\nu/d\mu)$ is in $\mathcal{H}(b)$, and
$$h = \frac{1-b}{1-u}V_u 1 = \frac{(1-b)(1-\overline{u(0)}u)}{(1-u)(1-\overline{u(0)})}.$$

Consider first a point λ in ∂D such that μ_λ is absolutely continuous. Then the operator $T_{1-\bar\lambda b}T_{\overline{F}_\lambda}$ is an isometry of H^2 onto $\mathcal{H}(b)$, so there is a function g_λ in H^2 such that $\|g_\lambda\|_2 = \|h\|_b$ and $h = T_{1-\bar\lambda b}T_{\overline{F}_\lambda}g_\lambda$. Then

$$\frac{F_\lambda}{1-u} = \frac{F_\lambda(1-\overline{u(0)})h}{(1-\overline{u(0)}u)(1-b)}$$
$$= \left(\frac{1-\overline{u(0)}}{1-\overline{u(0)}u}\right)\frac{(1-\bar\lambda b)F_\lambda}{1-b}T_{\overline{F}_\lambda}g_\lambda$$
$$= \left(\frac{1-\overline{u(0)}}{1-\overline{u(0)}u}\right)T_F T_{\overline{F}_\lambda}g_\lambda.$$

As shown in (IV-16), the operator $T_F T_{\overline{F}_\lambda}$ is bounded on H^2 with norm at most $2/|1-\lambda|$. We can conclude that $F_\lambda/(1-u)$ is in H^2, with norm at most $2\left(\dfrac{1+|u(0)|}{1-|u(0)|}\right)\|h\|_b/|1-\lambda|$. This settles the case where μ_λ is absolutely continuous, which accounts for almost every λ on ∂D. Because of the preceding norm estimate, the general case now follows by Fatou's lemma.

Notes

(NIV-1) The characterization of the extreme points of the unit ball of H^∞ in terms of log-integrability can be found in the book of K. Hoffman [35, p. 138].

(NIV-2) The paper [20] of Davis and McCarthy contains a characterization of the functions that are multipliers of $\mathcal{H}(b)$ for every nonextreme point b. They are the functions whose Taylor coefficients are $O(e^{-cn^{1/2}})$ for some positive constant c. These are precisely the functions in the dual of the Smirnov class in D (the space of ratios of H^∞ functions with outer denominators).

(NIV-3) The book [65] of B. Sz.–Nagy and C. Foias is the basic reference for their model theory. The Sz.–Nagy–Foias model for the operator X was worked out in a more plodding manner in the author's paper [58]. The case where b is extreme, treated in (V-6) below, is also given there. These results are special cases of those of Ball and Kriete [9], which deal with vector-valued de Branges–Rovnyak spaces and clarify the relation between the model theories of de Branges–Rovnyak and Sz.–Nagy Foias.

(NIV-4) The invariant subspaces of the operator X, when b is nonextreme, were found in the author's paper [59]. They are just the intersections of $\mathcal{H}(b)$ with the invariant subspaces of S^*, in other words, the subspaces $\mathcal{H}(b) \cap \mathcal{H}(u)$ with u inner (along with $\mathcal{H}(b)$ itself). The invariant subspace lattice of the operator $S|\mathcal{H}(b)$ can be more complicated. The case where $b(z) = \dfrac{1+z}{2}$ is worked out in [59].

(NIV-5) If $\|b\|_\infty < 1$ then, obviously, the functions F_λ are uniformly bounded in H^∞. The converse is also true. Namely, if $\|F_\lambda\|_\infty \leq c$ for all λ, then in D we have $|a| \leq c|1 - \overline{\lambda}b|$ for all λ, implying that $|a| \leq c(1 - |b|)$. Passing to ∂D, we can conclude that $1 - |b|^2 \leq c^2(1 - |b|)^2$, in other words, $(1 + |b|)/(1 - |b|) \leq c^2$, which implies that $\|b\|_\infty \leq (c^2 - 1)/(c^2 + 1)$.

When $\|b\|_\infty = 1$, it is still possible for every function F_λ to be in H^∞. This occurs, for example, for the function $b(z) = \dfrac{1+z}{2}$.

(NIV-6) The boundedness results in (IV-13), (IV-14) and (IV-15) suggest the problem of characterizing those pairs of H^2 functions φ and ψ for which the operator $T_\varphi T_{\overline{\psi}}$ is bounded. Some comments on this problem can be found in the author's paper [63]. D. Zheng [S18] has made recent progress.

(NIV-7) It would be interesting to have a converse to (IV-17). Specifically, let u be a nonconstant inner function and let ν be the measure on ∂D whose

Poisson integral is the real part of $\dfrac{1+u}{1-u}$. If $F/(1-u)$ is in H^2, is it true that there is a point λ in $\partial D\backslash\{1\}$ such that ν is absolutely continuous with respect to μ_λ, with $d\nu/d\mu_\lambda$ in $L^2(\mu_\lambda)$? The question is related to a conjecture about the structure of the exposed points of the unit ball in the space H^1; further details are in [63] and Chapter X. The result in question is true for the special case where $u(z) = z$, as one can see by combining propositions (VI-7) and (VI-9) below.

(NIV-8) For the statement in (IV-11) about the boundary behavior of the Poisson integral of a positive measure on ∂D, the reader is referred to [55, Theorem 7.5] and [27, p. 47], which give the analogous result for the derivative of a measure. The result for Poisson integrals is an easy consequence, as in [27, p. 77].

CHAPTER V

EXTREME POINTS

The character of $\mathcal{H}(b)$ when b is extreme is in certain respects the opposite of what it is when b is nonextreme. If b is extreme then (and only then) $H^2(\rho) = L^2(\rho)$, so the transformation K_ρ is an isometry of $L^2(\rho)$ onto $\mathcal{H}(\bar{b})$. We shall let b_0 be the outer factor and u_0 the inner factor of b.

Here are some of the contrasts between the extreme and nonextreme cases: If b is nonextreme then $\mathcal{H}(b)$ contains all functions that are holomorphic on $\overline{D}$, while if b is extreme the only such functions it contains are the rational functions in $\mathcal{H}(u_0)$. If b is nonextreme then it belongs to $\mathcal{H}(b)$, but it does not if it is extreme. If b is nonextreme then $\mathcal{H}(\bar{b})$ is dense in $\mathcal{H}(b)$, but for b extreme that density occurs if and only if b is an outer function.

Also in this chapter, the Sz.-Nagy-Foias model for the restricted backward shift in $\mathcal{H}(b)$ is worked out for the case where b is extreme, the spectrum of that operator is determined, and the absolute continuity criterion from Chapter III is adapted to the case where b is extreme.

(V-1) Noncontinuability. *If b is extreme, then no nonzero function in $\mathcal{H}(\bar{b})$ can be continued analytically across all of ∂D. The only functions in $\mathcal{H}(b)$ that can be continued analytically across all of ∂D are the rational functions in $\ker T_{\bar{b}}$.*

Suppose the function g in $\mathcal{H}(\bar{b})$ can be continued analytically across all of ∂D, and let q be the function in $L^2(\rho)$ such that $g = K_\rho q$. The last equality can be written $g = P_+(q\rho)$, because $q\rho \; (= q\rho^{1/2}\rho^{1/2})$ is in L^2. The function $q\rho$ is not log-integrable because

$$\log|q\rho| \leq \log^+ |q\rho^{1/2}| + \frac{1}{2}\log\rho$$

(the first term on the right side is integrable, but the second term has integral $-\infty$). However, the forward Fourier coefficients of $q\rho$ (the coefficients with positive indices) tend to 0 exponentially, because $P_+(q\rho)$ is the function

g, which was assumed to be analytically continuable across all of ∂D. It is known that, except for the zero function, there is no log-nonintegrable function in L^2 whose forward Fourier coefficients tend to 0 exponentially. (An explanation is given in (NV-1).) Hence $q\rho = 0$, and so also $g = 0$, which proves the first half of the proposition.

To prove the second half, suppose the function h in $\mathcal{H}(b)$ can be continued analytically across all of ∂D. It is asserted that the same is then true of $T_{\bar{b}}h$. In fact, the n-th Taylor coefficient of $T_{\bar{b}}h$ equals $\langle T_{\bar{b}}h, S^n 1\rangle$, which is the same as $\langle S^{*n}h, b\rangle$ and so is bounded in modulus by $\|S^{*n}h\|_2$. Since the Taylor coefficients of h tend to 0 exponentially, so do the norms $\|S^{*n}h\|_2$, as an easy estimate shows, and the assertion is established. Since $T_{\bar{b}}h$ is in $\mathcal{H}(\bar{b})$ (by II-4), it now follows by the first half of the proposition that $T_{\bar{b}}h = 0$. Then $T_{\bar{u}_0}h = 0$, in other words, h is in $\mathcal{H}(u_0)$; in particular, h is a noncyclic vector of S^*. Finally, it is known that a function holomorphic on $\overline{D}$ is a cyclic vector of S^* unless it is a rational function (a reference is given in (NV-3)). Hence h is a rational function, and this completes the proof of the proposition except for the remark that the functions in $\ker T_{\bar{b}}$, and in particular the rational functions in that kernel, are obviously in $\mathcal{H}(b)$.

(V-2) Cyclic Vectors. *If b is extreme, then the nonzero functions in $\mathcal{H}(\bar{b})$ are cyclic vectors of S^*. The only functions in $\mathcal{H}(b)$ that are noncyclic vectors of S^* are the functions in $\ker T_{\bar{b}}$.*

Suppose g is a nonzero function in $\mathcal{H}(\bar{b})$, and let q be the function in $L^2(\rho)$ such that $g = K_\rho q$. As in the preceding proof, we have $g = P_+(q\rho)$, and $q\rho$ fails to be log-integrable. Let M be the invariant subspace of S^* generated by g. The subspace $M + (H^2)^\perp$ is then an invariant subspace of the adjoint of the bilateral shift operator on L^2 (the operator of multiplication by the independent variable). It is known (a reference is given in (NV-2)) that the only invariant subspaces of the adjoint of the bilateral shift are the subspaces $v\overline{H}^2$, with v a unimodular function on ∂D, and the subspaces $\chi_E L^2$, with E a measurable subset of ∂D. The former possibility is precluded because $M + (H^2)^\perp$ contains the function $q\rho$, which is not log-integrable. Hence $M + (H^2)^\perp$ is of the latter form, and since it contains the function g, which is nonzero almost everywhere on ∂D, the corresponding set E must in fact be all of ∂D, in other words, $M + (H^2)^\perp = L^2$. Therefore $M = H^2$, which means g is a cyclic vector of S^*. This proves the first half of the proposition.

To prove the second half, suppose the function h in $\mathcal{H}(b)$ is noncyclic for

S^*. Then $T_{\bar b}h$ is noncyclic for S^* and it lies in $\mathcal{H}(\bar b)$, so $T_{\bar b}h = 0$ by the first half of the proposition, as desired.

(V-3) Noninclusion of b. Norm of S^*b. According to (IV-4), if b is nonextreme, then b belongs to $\mathcal{H}(b)$. We can now establish the converse. Namely, suppose b belongs to $\mathcal{H}(b)$. Then $T_{\bar b}b$ is in $\mathcal{H}(\bar b)$. Since

$$T_{\bar b}b = 1 - (1 - T_{\bar b}T_b)1,$$

it follows that the constant function 1 is in $\mathcal{H}(\bar b)$, which (by either (V-1) or (V-2)) implies b is nonextreme.

The formula $X^*h = Sh - \langle h, S^*b \rangle_b b$ from (II-9) together with the last result shows that $\mathcal{H}(b)$ fails to be S-invariant when b is extreme.

If we let S^* act on the expression above for $T_{\bar b}b$ we find that $T_{\bar b}S^*b = -S^*K_\rho 1$. Since K_ρ intertwines the operators S^* and Z_ρ^* (as shown in (III-3)), the last equality can be rewritten as $T_{\bar b}S^*b = -K_\rho Z_\rho^*1$. Consequently

$$\|S^*b\|_b^2 = \|S^*b\|_2^2 + \|T_{\bar b}S^*b\|_{\bar b}^2$$
$$= \|S^*b\|_2^2 + \|Z_\rho^*1\|_\rho^2.$$

If b is extreme then $H^2(\rho) = L^2(\rho)$, so that Z_ρ is a unitary operator. We then obtain

$$\|S^*b\|_b^2 = \|S^*b\|_2^2 + \|1\|_\rho^2$$
$$= \|b\|_2^2 - |b(0)|^2 + 1 - \|b\|_2^2$$
$$= 1 - |b(0)|^2.$$

(V-4) Orthogonal Decomposition. *If b is extreme, then $\mathcal{H}(b)$ is the orthogonal direct sum of $\mathcal{H}(b_0)$ and $b_0\mathcal{H}(u_0)$. The space $\mathcal{H}(b_0)$ is contained isometrically in $\mathcal{H}(b)$, and T_{b_0} acts as an isometry of $\mathcal{H}(u_0)$ into $\mathcal{H}(b)$.*

The equality $\mathcal{H}(b) = \mathcal{H}(b_0) + b_0\mathcal{H}(u_0)$ follows from (I-10), and the other statements follow from (I-11) in virtue of the triviality of $\mathcal{H}(b_0) \cap b_0\mathcal{H}(u_0)$, which is a consequence of (V-2) together with (II-5).

(V-5) Closure of $\mathcal{H}(\bar b)$ in $\mathcal{H}(b)$. *If b is extreme then the closure of $\mathcal{H}(\bar b)$ in $\mathcal{H}(b)$ is $\mathcal{H}(b_0)$. Hence, $\mathcal{H}(\bar b)$ is dense in $\mathcal{H}(b)$ if and only if b is an outer function.*

Since $\mathcal{H}(\bar b)$ is the same as $\mathcal{H}(\bar b_0)$, it is contained in $\mathcal{H}(b_0)$. Since $\mathcal{H}(b_0)$ is closed in $\mathcal{H}(b)$ by (V-4), the closure of $\mathcal{H}(\bar b)$ in $\mathcal{H}(b)$ is contained in $\mathcal{H}(b_0)$. By

(V-4), it only remains to show that every function in $\mathcal{H}(b)$ that is orthogonal to $\mathcal{H}(\bar{b})$ belongs to $b_0 \mathcal{H}(u_0)$.

Let the function h in $\mathcal{H}(b)$ be orthogonal to $\mathcal{H}(\bar{b})$, and let s be the function in $L^2(\rho)$ such that $T_{\bar{b}} h = K_\rho s$. Let g be any function in $\mathcal{H}(\bar{b})$, and let q be the function in $L^2(\rho)$ such that $g = K_\rho q$. By (III-5) we have $T_{\bar{b}} g = K_\rho \bar{b} q$. Hence

$$\begin{aligned} 0 &= \langle h, g \rangle_b \\ &= \langle h, g \rangle + \langle T_{\bar{b}} h, T_{\bar{b}} g \rangle_{\bar{b}} \\ &= \langle h, K_\rho q \rangle + \langle s, \bar{b} q \rangle_\rho. \end{aligned}$$

The first term on the right equals $\langle h, P_+(q\rho) \rangle$, which is the same as $\langle h, q\rho \rangle$, in other words, $\langle h, q \rangle_\rho$. We thus obtain

$$\langle h + bs, q \rangle_\rho = 0.$$

This must hold for all q in $L^2(\rho)$ (this is where the assumption that b is extreme becomes essential), and therefore $h + bs$ is the zero function in $L^2(\rho)$. Consequently

$$(1 - |b|^2) h + (1 - |b|^2) bs = 0,$$

which can be written

$$\frac{h}{b} = \bar{b} h - (1 - |b|^2) s.$$

It follows that the function h/b is in L^2. Applying the projection P_+ to the preceding equality, and recalling that $T_{\bar{b}} h = K_\rho s \ (= P_+(\rho s))$, we find that $P_+(h/b) = 0$, in other words, h/b is orthogonal to H^2. However h/b_0 is in H^2 because it is in L^2 and b_0 is an outer function. Thus $T_{\bar{u}_0}(h/b_0) = 0$, in other words, h/b_0 is in $\mathcal{H}(u_0)$, which is the desired conclusion.

(V-6) Sz–Nagy–Foias Model of X. Assume b is extreme. The map $h \mapsto h \oplus K_\rho^{-1} T_{\bar{b}} h$ is then an isometry of $\mathcal{H}(b)$ into $H^2 \oplus L^2(\rho)$ (by (II-4) and (III-2)). The range of this isometry consists of all vectors $f \oplus q$ in $H^2 \oplus L^2(\rho)$ such that $T_{\bar{b}} f = K_\rho q$, in other words, it is the kernel of the operator $[T_{\bar{b}} \ - K_\rho]$ from $H^2 \oplus L^2(\rho)$ to H^2. The preceding operator is the adjoint of the operator

$$B = \begin{bmatrix} T_b \\ -J_\rho \end{bmatrix}$$

from H^2 to $H^2 \oplus L^2(\rho)$, which is easily seen to be an isometry. (Recall from (III-2) that J_ρ is the natural injection of H^2 into $L^2(\rho)$.) The image of $\mathcal{H}(b)$ under the isometry above is thus equal to $\mathcal{H}(B)$, and, letting Q denote the projection in $H^2 \oplus L^2(\rho)$ onto the first coordinate space, we can conclude that Q gives an isometry of $\mathcal{H}(B)$ onto $\mathcal{H}(b)$. (One can obtain the last conclusion more directly by computing $1 - BB^*$—it is a two-by-two operator matrix—and noting that the upper-left entry is $1 - T_b T_{\bar b}$.)

From (III-3) one sees that the operator $Q|\mathcal{H}(B)$ intertwines the operators $(S^* \oplus Z_\rho^*)|\mathcal{H}(B)$ and X. The former operator is thus the Sz.–Nagy–Foias model of the latter one.

(V-7) Spectral Points of X in D. *Assume b is extreme, and let w be a point of D. Then $\overline{w}$ is in the spectrum of the operator X if and only if $b(w) = 0$.*

In fact, from the intertwining relation (III-8) we know that X is unitarily equivalent to a rank-one perturbation of the operator Z_μ^*, which is unitary. By Fredholm theory, therefore, any spectral point of X in D must be an eigenvalue. But X is just the restriction of S^* to $\mathcal{H}(b)$, and the eigenspace of S^* for the eigenvalue $\overline{w}$ is the one-dimensional subspace spanned by the kernel function k_w. Hence $\overline{w}$ is in the spectrum of X if and only if k_w is in $\mathcal{H}(b)$. By (V-2), the latter happens if and only if $b(w) = 0$.

We can go a little further and obtain an explicit expression for $(X - \overline{w})^{-1}$ when $b(w) \neq 0$. First we note that, for h in $\mathcal{H}(b)$,

$$XX^*h = S^*(Sh - \langle h, S^*b\rangle_b b)$$
$$= h - \langle h, S^*b\rangle_b S^*b,$$

in other words, $XX^* = 1 - (S^*b \otimes S^*b)$. Using the equality $(X - \overline{w})k_w^b = -\overline{b(w)}S^*b$, obtained (with slightly different notation) in (II-9), we can rewrite this as

$$XX^* = 1 + (X - \overline{w})\overline{b(w)}^{-1}(k_w^b \otimes S^*b),$$

and hence as

$$(X - \overline{w})\Big(X^* - \overline{b(w)}^{-1}(k_w^b \otimes S^*b)\Big) = 1 - \overline{w}X^*.$$

It follows that

$$(X - \overline{w})^{-1} = \Big(X^* - \overline{b(w)}^{-1}(k_w^b \otimes S^*b)\Big)(1 - \overline{w}X^*)^{-1}.$$

Since $(1 - wX)^{-1}S^*b$ is the function $Q_w b$ introduced in (II-8), the preceding expression can be rewritten as

$$(X - \overline{w})^{-1} = X^*(1 - \overline{w}X^*)^{-1} - \overline{b(w)}^{-1}(k_w^b \otimes Q_w b).$$

(V-8) Spectral Points of X on ∂D. *Assume b is extreme, and let I be an open subarc of ∂D. The following conditions are equivalent.*

(i) *I is contained in the resolvent set of X^*.*

(ii) *Every function in $\mathcal{H}(b)$ can be continued analytically across I.*

(iii) *The function b can be continued analytically across I, and its continuation has unit modulus on I.*

To prove that condition (i) implies condition (ii) we shall use the formula $k_w^b = (1 - \overline{w}X^*)^{-1}k_0^b$, which is an easy consequence of the analogous formula in H^2, namely, $k_w = (1 - \overline{w}S)^{-1}k_0$. In fact, for h in $\mathcal{H}(b)$ we have

$$h(w) = \langle h, (1 - \overline{w}S)^{-1}k_0 \rangle = \langle (1 - wS^*)^{-1}h, k_0 \rangle$$
$$= \langle (1 - wX)^{-1}h, k_0^b \rangle_b = \langle h, (1 - \overline{w}X^*)^{-1}k_0^b \rangle_b,$$

as desired. Now if I is contained in the resolvent set of X^* then the expression on the right side of the preceding string of equalities, thought of as a function of w, can be continued analytically across I, and so condition (ii) is satisfied.

Suppose condition (ii) holds. Then, in particular, the function S^*b can be continued analytically across I, and therefore so can b. Moreover, if w_0 is a point of I, then an application of the principle of uniform boundedness shows that the functional on $\mathcal{H}(b)$ of evaluation at w_0 is bounded; let $k_{w_0}^b$ denote the corresponding kernel function. The functions k_w^b obviously tend weakly to $k_{w_0}^b$ as w tends to w_0 from D. Thus, for z in D we have

$$k_{w_0}^b(z) = \langle k_{w_0}^b, k_z^b \rangle_b$$
$$= \lim_{w \to w_0} \langle k_w^b, k_z^b \rangle_b$$
$$= \lim_{w \to w_0} \frac{1 - \overline{b(w)}b(z)}{1 - \overline{w}z}$$
$$= \frac{1 - \overline{b(w_0)}b(z)}{1 - \overline{w_0}z}.$$

In particular, then, the function $\dfrac{1 - \overline{b(w_0)}b(z)}{1 - \overline{w_0}z}$ is in H^2, which is only possible if $|b(w_0)| = 1$. We can conclude that condition (iii) holds.

Suppose finally that condition (iii) holds. Then from standard properties of the Poisson integral one can conclude that the part of the measure μ carried by I is purely atomic, with atoms situated at the points of I where b takes the value 1. The essential spectrum of the operator Z_μ is thus disjoint from I. Since X^* is unitarily equivalent to a rank-one perturbation of Z_μ, it has the same property. Thus X has the same property relative to the arc I^* (the set of complex conjugates of points in I). Any spectral point of X on I^* must thus be an eigenvalue. Because S^* has no eigenvalues on ∂D, we can conclude that I^* is contained in the resolvent set of X, in other words, condition (i) is satisfied.

(V-9) Comparison of Measures. *Let b be extreme, let u be a nonconstant inner function, and let ν be the measure on ∂D whose Poisson integral is the real part of $\dfrac{1+u}{1-u}$. The following conditions are equivalent:*

(i) *ν is absolutely continuous with respect to μ, and $\dfrac{d\nu}{d\mu}$ is in $L^2(\mu)$;*

(ii) *the function $\dfrac{1-b}{1-u}$ is in H^2, and the function $\dfrac{1}{1-u}$ is in $L^2(\rho)$.*

Because of (III-11), it will be enough to show that condition (ii) holds if and only if the function $\left(\dfrac{1-b}{1-u}\right) k_0^u$ belongs to $\mathcal{H}(b)$.

Suppose (ii) holds. Then

$$T_{\bar{b}}\left(\left(\frac{1-b}{1-u}\right) k_0^u\right) = P_+\left(\frac{\bar{b}-|b|^2}{1-u}(1-\overline{u(0)}u)\right)$$

$$= P_+\left(\frac{1-|b|^2}{1-u}(1-\overline{u(0)}u)\right) + P_+\left(\frac{\bar{b}-1}{\bar{u}-1}(\bar{u}-\overline{u(0)})\right).$$

The second term on the right is 0, and the first term is $K_\rho\left(\dfrac{1-\overline{u(0)}u}{1-u}\right)$.

Hence $T_{\bar{b}}\left(\left(\dfrac{1-b}{1-u}\right) k_0^u\right)$ is in $\mathcal{H}(\bar{b})$, and so $\left(\dfrac{1-b}{1-u}\right) k_0^u$ is in $\mathcal{H}(b)$, as desired.

Suppose, conversely, that $\left(\dfrac{1-b}{1-u}\right) k_0^u$ is in $\mathcal{H}(b)$. Let q be the function in $L^2(\rho)$ such that $T_{\bar{b}}\left(\dfrac{1-b}{1-u}\right) k_0^u = K_\rho q$. By the reasoning above we also have

$$T_{\bar{b}}\left(\left(\frac{1-b}{1-u}\right) k_0^u\right) = P_+\left(\frac{1-|b|^2}{1-u}(1-\overline{u(0)}u)\right).$$

Hence
$$P_+\left(\left(\frac{1-\overline{u(0)}u}{1-u}-q\right)\rho\right)=0.$$

It is asserted that the function $\left(\dfrac{1-\overline{u(0)}u}{1-u}-q\right)\rho$ is not log-integrable. That together with the preceding equality will imply that the function vanishes, in other words, that $\dfrac{1-\overline{u(0)}u}{1-u}=q$ almost everywhere on the set where ρ is nonzero. The desired conclusion, that $\dfrac{1}{1-u}$ is in $L^2(\rho)$, will follow.

The asserted log-nonintegrability holds because the logarithm of the absolute value of the function in question is bounded from above by

$$\log\left(\frac{2}{|1-u|}+|q|\rho^{1/2}\right)+\frac{1}{2}\log\rho,$$

which in turn is bounded from above by

$$\log^+\frac{4}{|1-u|}+\log^+|q|\rho^{1/2}+\frac{1}{2}\log\rho.$$

Each of the first two terms in the preceding expression is integrable, and the integral of the last term is $-\infty$, so the assertion follows.

Notes

(NV-1) A proof of the log-integrability of a nonzero L^2 function whose forward Fourier coefficients tend to 0 exponentially can be found in [56, p. 12]. The main point is that such a function is the inner boundary function of a function in H^2 of a suitably small annulus centered at 0 with ∂D as its inner boundary.

(NV-2) The classification of the invariant subspaces of the bilateral shift operator on L^2 can be found in K. Hoffman's book [35, p. 111].

(NV-3) The cyclic and noncyclic vectors of the backward shift, S^*, are studied in the paper [23] of R. G. Douglas, H. S. Shapiro and A. L. Shields. Those authors obtain a characterization of the noncyclic vectors in terms of pseudocontinuation. A proof that a function holomorphic on $\overline{D}$ is cyclic for S^* unless it is rational can be found in their paper.

(NV-4) The results in (V-7) and (V-8) about the spectrum of X when b is extreme are very special cases of a theorem of Sz.–Nagy and Foias [65, p. 259] about the spectra of their model operators.

(NV-5) Proposition (V-9) on comparison of measures is true word for word when b is nonextreme; that version is just (IV-8). However, a unified proof of the two cases is lacking.

(NV-6) F. D. Suárez [S17] has classified the invariant subspaces of the restricted backward shift in $\mathcal{H}(b)$ for the case where b is extreme.

CHAPTER VI

ANGULAR DERIVATIVES

The spaces $\mathcal{H}(b)$ enable one to give a Hilbert space approach to C. Carathéodory's theorem on angular derivatives and the fixed-point theorem of A. Denjoy and J. Wolff. The usual approach to Carathéodory's theorem has a strongly geometric character. It is based on Schwarz's lemma and on a boundary version of Schwarz's lemma known as Julia's lemma. The recent monograph [S13] of J. H. Shapiro contains a lucid account. The Hilbert space approach, while submerging the geometric underpinnings of the theorem, affords insight from a different perspective. In this treatment, Julia's lemma emerges as a consequence of Schwarz's inequality.

After a little background on angular derivatives, the notion of an angular derivative in the sense of Carathéodory will be introduced, and Carathéodory's theorem will be proved. Then several equivalent conditions for the existence of an angular derivative in the sense of Carathéodory will be derived, and the Denjoy-Wolff theorems on fixed points and iteration will be established.

(VI-1) Angular Derivatives. *For a holomorphic function f in D and a point z_0 of ∂D, the following conditions are equivalent*

(i) The function f has a nontangential limit, $f(z_0)$, at the point z_0, and the difference quotient $(f(z) - f(z_0))/(z - z_0)$ has a nontangential limit at z_0.

(ii) The derivative f' has a nontangential limit at z_0.

When these conditions hold, one says that f has an angular derivative at z_0. Then, as will be shown in the proof to follow, the nontangential limit at z_0 of the difference quotient equals the nontangential limit of the derivative; that number is called the angular derivative of f at z_0 and denoted by $f'(z_0)$. In regard to condition (i), note that it is implied by a slight weakening of itself: if there is any complex number λ such that $\dfrac{f(z) - \lambda}{z - z_0}$ has a nontangential limit at z_0, then λ must clearly be the nontangential limit of f at z_0, so that (i) holds.

To prove the proposition, suppose first that condition (ii) holds. We can then define $f(z_0)$ to be $f(0) + \int_{[0,z_0]} f'(\zeta)d\zeta$. An application of Cauchy's theorem shows that, if z is any point of D, then $f(z_0) = f(z) + \int_{[z,z_0]} f'(\zeta)d\zeta$. Hence, letting $f'(z_0)$ denote the nontangential limit of f' at z_0, we have

$$\frac{f(z) - f(z_0)}{z - z_0} = \frac{1}{z - z_0} \int_{[z_0,z]} f'(\zeta) d\zeta$$

$$= f'(z_0) + \frac{1}{z - z_0} \int_{[z_0,z]} [f'(\zeta) - f'(z_0)]d\zeta.$$

As z tends nontangentially to z_0 the last term on the right side tends to 0, and so condition (i) holds.

Assume, conversely, that condition (i) holds, and let $f'(z_0)$ denote the nontangential limit of the difference quotient at z_0. Fix a nontangential approach region at z_0, say the region

$$R_K = \{z \in D : |z - z_0| \leq K(1 - |z|)\},$$

where K is a positive constant. For z in R_K let γ_z denote the circle with center z and radius $\frac{1}{2}(1 - |z|)$. A simple estimate shows that γ_z then lies within the region R_{2K+1}. For $0 < \varepsilon < 1$ define the number $\alpha(\varepsilon)$ by

$$\alpha(\varepsilon) = \sup\left\{\left|\frac{f(\zeta) - f(z_0)}{\zeta - z_0} - f'(z_0)\right| : \zeta \in R_{2K+1}, |\zeta - z_0| < \varepsilon\right\};$$

this quantity tends to 0 with ε. For z in R_K we use Cauchy's formula for the derivative:

$$f'(z) = \frac{1}{2\pi i} \int_{\gamma_z} \frac{f(\zeta)}{(\zeta - z)^2} d\zeta.$$

Writing $f(\zeta) = f(z_0) + f'(z_0)(\zeta - z_0) + \beta(\zeta)(\zeta - z_0)$, we have the estimate $|\beta(\zeta)| \leq \alpha(|\zeta - z_0|) \leq \alpha\left(\frac{3}{2}|z - z_0|\right)$ for ζ on γ_z, and

$$f'(z) = f'(z_0) + \frac{1}{2\pi i} \int_{\gamma_z} \frac{\beta(\zeta)(\zeta - z_0)}{(\zeta - z)^2} d\zeta.$$

The integrand in the preceding integral is bounded in modulus by

$$\alpha\left(\frac{3}{2}|z - z_0|\right)\left(\frac{1}{2}(1 - |z|) + |z - z_0|\right)\frac{1}{4}(1 - |z|)^2,$$

which is no larger than

$$(2 + 4K)\alpha\left(\frac{3}{2}|z - z_0|\right)(1 - |z|).$$

Hence the integral itself is bounded in modulus by $(1 + 2K)\alpha\left(\frac{3}{2}|z - z_0|\right)$, which tends to 0 as $z \to z_0$. This proves that $f'(z)$ tends to $f'(z_0)$ as z tends to z_0 from within R_K, in other words, condition (ii) holds.

(VI-2) Angular Derivatives in the Sense of Carathéodory. This notion applies to holomorphic self-maps of D (such as our function b). One says that such a function has an angular derivative in the sense of Carathéodory at the point z_0 of ∂D if it has an angular derivative at z_0 and if its nontangential limit at z_0 has unit modulus.

(VI-3) Carathéodory's Theorem. *If z_0 is a point of ∂D and*

$$(C) \qquad c = \liminf_{z \to z_0} \frac{1 - |b(z)|}{1 - |z|} < \infty,$$

then b has an angular derivative in the sense of Carathéodory at z_0. The relation $b'(z_0) = cb(z_0)/z_0$ holds, and $\dfrac{1-|b(z)|}{1-|z|}$ tends to c as z tends nontangentially to z_0. The number c is positive.

In the other direction, if b has an angular derivative in the sense of Carathéodory at z_0, then $\dfrac{1-|b(z)|}{1-|z|}$ obviously stays bounded as z tends to z_0 radially, so that condition (C) holds.

(VI-4) Hilbert Space Version. *For z_0 a point of ∂D, the following conditions are equivalent.*

(i) Condition (C) above.

(ii) There is a complex number λ of unit modulus such that the function $\dfrac{b(z) - \lambda}{z - z_0}$ is in $\mathcal{H}(b)$.

(iii) Every function in $\mathcal{H}(b)$ has a nontangential limit at the point z_0.

Two comments are in order prior to the proofs. First, if condition (ii) holds then the number λ must be the nontangential limit of b at z_0. In fact, because every H^2 function is $o((1-|z|)^{-1/2})$ as $|z| \to 1$, it follows from (ii) that $b(z) = \lambda + (z-z_0)o((1-|z|)^{-1/2})$, and the last term on the right tends to 0 as z tends to z_0 nontangentially (even as z tends to z_0 oricyclically). Second, if conditions (ii) and (iii) hold then, by applying (iii) to the function $\dfrac{b(z) - \lambda}{z - z_0}$, one sees that b has an angular derivative in the sense of Carathéodory at z_0. Thus, each of the conditions (i)–(iii) is equivalent to the existence for b of an angular derivative in the sense of Carathéodory at z_0.

(VI-5) Proofs. Suppose to begin that condition (C) holds. The key to the Hilbert space approach to Carathéodory's theorem is the observation that the constant c can be re-expressed as

$$c = \liminf_{z \to z_0} \|k_z^b\|_b^2.$$

Hence, there is a sequence $(z_n)_1^\infty$ in D tending to z_0 such that $\|k_{z_n}^b\|_b^2$ tends to c. We can assume the sequence $(b(z_n))_1^\infty$ converges, say to λ, and, because closed balls in a Hilbert space are weakly compact, that the sequence $(k_{z_n}^b)_1^\infty$ converges weakly in $\mathcal{H}(b)$, say to the function h. Then, for any point z in D,

$$h(z) = \langle h, k_z^b \rangle_b = \lim_{n \to \infty} \langle k_{z_n}^b, k_z^b \rangle_b$$
$$= \lim_{n \to \infty} \frac{1 - \overline{b(z_n)}b(z)}{1 - \overline{z_n}z} = \frac{1 - \overline{\lambda}b(z)}{1 - \overline{z_0}z}.$$

The function on the right side cannot belong to H^2 if $|\lambda| < 1$, so we must have $|\lambda| = 1$, and thus condition (VI-4)(ii) holds. Note also that $\|h\|_b^2 \leq c$, which proves $c > 0$ (as asserted in (VI-3)).

Suppose next that condition (VI-4)(ii) holds. As noted earlier, the number λ must be the nontangential limit of b at z_0, so we shall denote it by $b(z_0)$. Also, we shall denote the function $\dfrac{1 - \overline{b(z_0)}b(z)}{1 - \overline{z_0}z}$ by $k_{z_0}^b$. To prove that condition (VI-4)(iii) holds it will be enough to prove that k_z^b tends to $k_{z_0}^b$ weakly as z tends nontangentially to z_0. Obviously $k_z^b \to k_{z_0}^b$ pointwise, in other words, $\langle k_z^b, k_w^b \rangle_b \to \langle k_{z_0}^b, k_w^b \rangle_b$ for each w in D as z tends nontangentially to z_0. Since the functions k_w^b span $\mathcal{H}(b)$, it will thus be enough to show that $\|k_z^b\|_b$ stays bounded as z tends nontangentially to z_0. For z in D we have

$$\langle k_{z_0}^b, k_z^b \rangle_b = \frac{1 - \overline{b(z_0)}b(z)}{1 - \overline{z_0}z},$$

so, by Schwarz's inequality,

$$\frac{|1 - \overline{b(z_0)}b(z)|^2}{|1 - \overline{z_0}z|^2} \leq \|k_{z_0}^b\|_b^2 \|k_z^b\|_b^2 = \|k_{z_0}^b\|_b^2 \left(\frac{1 - |b(z)|^2}{1 - |z|^2} \right).$$

In the preceding inequality, the numerator on the left side majorizes $(1 - |b(z)|)^2$, so we get

$$\frac{(1 - |b(z)|)^2}{|z - z_0|^2} \leq \|k_{z_0}^b\|_b^2 \left(\frac{1 - |b(z)|^2}{1 - |z|^2} \right),$$

which implies that

$$\|k_z^b\|_b^2 = \frac{1 - |b(z)|^2}{1 - |z|^2}$$
$$\leq \|k_{z_0}^b\|_b^2 \left(\frac{1 + |b(z)|}{1 + |z|} \right)^2 \left(\frac{|z - z_0|}{1 - |z|} \right)^2.$$

Since the right side here stays bounded as z tends nontangentially to z_0, the desired conclusion follows. This completes the proof that condition (VI-4)(ii) implies condition (VI-4)(iii).

To complete the circle of implications it suffices to note that if condition (VI-4)(iii) holds then, by the principle of uniform boundedness, the norms $\|k_z^b\|_b$ stay bounded as z tends nontangentially to z_0, so condition (C) is satisfied. This finishes the proof of (VI-4).

To finish the proof of (VI-3), we assume condition (C) holds, and we retain the notations introduced above. The angular derivative $b'(z_0)$ is the nontangential limit of $\dfrac{b(z) - b(z_0)}{z - z_0}$ at z_0. Since

$$\frac{b(z) - b(z_0)}{z - z_0} = \langle k_{z_0}^b, k_z^b \rangle_b \, b(z_0)/z_0,$$

and since k_z^b tends weakly to $k_{z_0}^b$ as z tends nontangentially to z_0, we have $b'(z_0) = \|k_{z_0}^b\|_b^2 b(z_0)/z_0$. It will be shown that $\|k_z^b\|_b$ tends to $\|k_{z_0}^b\|_b$ as z tends nontangentially to z_0. It will follow that $\|k_{z_0}^b\|_b^2 \geq c$, and since the opposite inequality is also true (as noted earlier), the equality $\|k_{z_0}^b\|_b^2 = c$ will follow. The expression above for $b'(z_0)$ will thus become $b'(z_0) = cb(z_0)/z_0$, and also the nontangential convergence of $\dfrac{1 - |b(z)|}{1 - |z|}$ at z_0 to c will follow, so the proof of (VI-3) will be complete.

To establish the nontangential convergence of $\|k_z^b\|_b$ to $\|k_{z_0}^b\|_b$ at z_0 we note that, as z tends nontangentially to z_0 we have

$$b(z) = b(z_0) + b'(z_0)(z - z_0) + o(|z - z_0|)$$
$$= b(z_0)[1 - \|k_{z_0}^b\|_b^2(1 - \bar{z}_0 z) + o(|z - z_0|)].$$

It follows that

$$|b(z)|^2 = 1 - 2\|k_{z_0}^b\|_b^2 \operatorname{Re}(1 - \bar{z}_0 z) + o(|z - z_0|)$$

as z tends nontangentially to z_0, so

$$\|k_z^b\|_b^2 = \frac{1 - |b(z)|^2}{1 - |z|^2} = 2\|k_{z_0}^b\|_b^2 \frac{\operatorname{Re}(1 - \bar{z}_0 z)}{1 - |z|^2} + \frac{o(|z - z_0|)}{1 - |z|^2}$$

as z tends nontangentially to z_0. The desired conclusion now follows, because as z tends nontangentially to z_0 the ratio $\operatorname{Re}(1 - \bar{z}_0 z)/(1 - |z|^2)$ tends to $1/2$, and the ratio $|z - z_0|/(1 - |z|^2)$ stays bounded.

Notice that the nontangential convergence of $\|k_z^b\|_b$ to $\|k_{z_0}^b\|_b$ at z_0, together with the weak convergence of k_z^b to $k_{z_0}^b$ as z tends nontangentially to z_0, implies that k_z^b actually tends to $k_{z_0}^b$ in norm as z tends nontangentially to z_0.

(VI-6) **Julia's Lemma.** *If condition (C) holds, then*

$$\frac{|b(z) - b(z_0)|^2}{1 - |b(z)|^2} \leq c \left(\frac{|z - z_0|^2}{1 - |z|^2} \right)$$

in D. The inequality is strict except when b is a Möbius transformation of D onto D.

In geometric terms the inequality says that, for $s > 0$, the interior of the circle of radius $\dfrac{s}{1+s}$ internally tangent to ∂D at the point z_0 is mapped by b into the interior of the circle of radius $\dfrac{cs}{1+cs}$ internally tangent to ∂D at the point $b(z_0)$.

After what has been shown above, we can rewrite the inequality in Julia's lemma as $|\langle k_{z_0}^b, k_z^b \rangle_b|^2 \leq \|k_{z_0}^b\|_b^2 \|k_z^b\|_b^2$; it is thus just an instance of Schwarz's inequality. (It was in fact used in the proof of (VI-3).) To obtain the condition for equality, one rewrites the inequality as

$$\mathrm{Re} \left[\frac{b(z_0) + b(z)}{b(z_0) - b(z)} - \frac{1}{c} \left(\frac{z_0 + z}{z_0 - z} \right) \right] \geq 0.$$

Since a nonnegative harmonic function in D is either positive everywhere or identically 0, the equality can hold at some point only if it holds throughout D, in which case the function in square brackets is an imaginary constant. One easily sees that b is then a Möbius transformation of D onto D. A simple argument shows that equality holds when b is such a Möbius transformation. (The condition for equality in Julia's lemma can also be derived from the condition for equality in Schwarz's inequality, but that argument is more complicated than the preceding one.)

(VI-7) **Angular Derivatives and Mass Points.** *The function b has an angular derivative in the sense of Carathéodory at the point z_0 of ∂D if and only if there is a point λ in ∂D such that the measure μ_λ has an atom at z_0. In that case $\lambda = b(z_0)$ and $\mu_\lambda(\{z_0\}) = 1/|b'(z_0)|$.*

Because of (VI-4), this is an immediate consequence of (III-12), except for the equality involving $|b'(z_0)|$. To establish that equality, assume μ_λ

has an atom at z_0. As z tends radially to z_0, the functions $(1 - |z|)k_z$ stay uniformly bounded and converge pointwise on ∂D to the characteristic function of the singleton $\{z_0\}$. The square of their norms in $L^2(\mu_\lambda)$ thus converge to $\mu_\lambda(\{z_0\})$. The norm of $(1 - |z|)k_z$ in $L^2(\mu_\lambda)$ is the same as the norm in $\mathcal{H}(b)$ of its image under the transformation $V_{\bar{\lambda}b}$. That image is

$$(1 - |z|)(1 - \lambda\overline{b(z)})^{-1}k_z^b,$$

the square of whose norm in $\mathcal{H}(b)$ is

$$\frac{(1 - |z|)^2(1 - |b(z)|^2)}{|b(z) - b(z_0)|^2(1 - |z|^2)}$$

(since $\lambda = b(z_0)$). As z tends radially to z_0, the last quantity tends (by (VI-3)) to $1/|b'(z_0)|$.

(VI-8) Another Criterion. In combination with (IV-8) and (V-9), the preceding criterion yields the following one: *The function b has an angular derivative at the point z_0 of ∂D if and only if there is a point λ in ∂D such that the functions $\dfrac{|b - \lambda|^2}{|z - z_0|^2}$ and $\dfrac{1 - |b|^2}{|z - z_0|^2}$ are in L^1.* Since $|b - \lambda|^2 + 1 - |b|^2 = 2\operatorname{Re}(1 - \bar{\lambda}b)$, and $|z - z_0|^2 = 2\operatorname{Re}(1 - \bar{z}_0 z)$ on ∂D, the last condition holds if and only if $\dfrac{\operatorname{Re}(1 - \bar{\lambda}b)}{\operatorname{Re}(1 - \bar{z}_0 z)}$ is in L^1.

(VI-9) Angular Derivatives and Square Integrability. If b has an angular derivative in the sense of Carathéodory at the point z_0 of ∂D then, for λ in $\partial D \setminus \{b(z_0)\}$,

$$\int_{\partial D} |e^{i\theta} - z_0|^{-2} d\mu_\lambda(e^{i\theta}) = |b'(z_0)||\lambda - b(z_0)|^{-2}.$$

The proof is similar to the preceding one. As z tends to z_0 radially, the functions zk_z increase in modulus on ∂D, so by the monotone convergence theorem the square of their $L^2(\mu_\lambda)$-norms converge to the integral on the left side of the equality above. The $L^2(\mu_\lambda)$-norm of zk_z equals the $\mathcal{H}(b)$-norm of the image of zk_z under $V_{\bar{\lambda}b}$, which is $z(1 - \lambda\overline{b(z)})^{-1}k_z^b$. The square of the $L^2(\mu_\lambda)$ norm of zk_z is thus $|z|^2|\lambda - b(z)|^{-2}\|k_z^b\|_b^2$ which, by (VI-3), tends to the right side of the equality above as z tends to z_0 radially.

(VI-10) Square Integrability and Angular Derivatives. *If, for the point z_0 in ∂D, there is a point λ in ∂D such that $\int_{\partial D} |e^{i\theta} - z_0|^{-2} d\mu_\lambda(e^{i\theta}) < \infty$, then b has an angular derivative in the sense of Carathéodory at z_0.*

The proof is a slight reworking of the preceding one. By the reasoning there, for z in D,

$$|z|^2 \|k_z^b\|_b^2 = |\lambda - b(z)|^2 \int_{\partial D} |z|^2 |e^{i\theta} - z|^{-2} d\mu_\lambda(e^{i\theta}).$$

As z tends radially to z_0, the integrands in the preceding integral increase monotonically to $|e^{i\theta} - z_0|^{-2}$, so, under the present hypothesis, the integrals stay bounded. Thus $\|k_z^b\|_b$ stays bounded as z tends radially to z_0, which says that condition (C) holds and hence that b has an angular derivative in the sense of Carathéodory at z_0.

(VI-11) Fixed Points. It is a well-known consequence of Schwarz's lemma that, unless b is the identity function, it can have at most one fixed point in D, and if z_0 is such a fixed point, then $|b'(z_0)| \leq 1$, the equality holding if and only if b is an elliptic Möbius transformation of D onto D (that is, a Möbius transformation that is conjugate, in the group of all Möbius transformations of D onto D, to a rotation). If $\|b\|_\infty < 1$ then b does have a fixed point in D. (This is everyone's favorite application of Rouché's theorem.)

A point z_0 on ∂D will be called a fixed point of b if b has the nontangential limit z_0 at z_0. If that happens, and if b has an angular derivative at z_0, then that angular derivative is positive, by (VI-3).

A fixed point z_0 of b will be called a Denjoy–Wolff point of b if it is in D or if it is on ∂D and b has an angular derivative there satisfying $b'(z_0) \leq 1$. Unless b is the identity function, it can have at most one such point. In fact, suppose z_0 and z_1 are distinct Denjoy–Wolff points of b. As noted above, Schwarz's lemma guarantees z_0 and z_1 are not both in D unless b is the identity function. Suppose z_1 is in D and z_0 is on ∂D. Then, for the determinant of the Grammian matrix of the two kernel functions $k_{z_0}^b$ and $k_{z_1}^b$ we have

$$0 \leq \det \begin{bmatrix} k_{z_0}^b(z_0) & k_{z_0}^b(z_1) \\ k_{z_1}^b(z_0) & k_{z_1}^b(z_1) \end{bmatrix} = \det \begin{bmatrix} b'(z_0) & 1 \\ 1 & 1 \end{bmatrix}$$

$$= b'(z_0) - 1 \leq 0,$$

so the determinant vanishes, which implies that $k_{z_0}^b$ and $k_{z_1}^b$ are linearly dependent, say $k_{z_1}^b = \alpha k_{z_0}^b$, where α is a constant. Then $k_{z_1}^b(z_1) = \alpha k_{z_0}^b(z_1)$, implying that actually $\alpha = 1$, and so

$$\frac{1 - \overline{z}_1 b(z)}{1 - \overline{z}_1 z} = \frac{1 - \overline{z}_0 b(z)}{1 - \overline{z}_0 z}.$$

The last equality implies b is the identity function. Suppose on the other hand that z_0 and z_1 are both on ∂D. Then, arguing as before, we have

$$0 \leq \det \begin{bmatrix} k_{z_0}^b(z_0) & k_{z_0}^b(z_1) \\ k_{z_1}^b(z_0) & k_{z_1}^b(z_1) \end{bmatrix} = \begin{bmatrix} b'(z_0) & 1 \\ 1 & b'(z_1) \end{bmatrix}$$

$$= b'(z_0) b'(z_1) - 1 \leq 0,$$

so again the determinant vanishes, and the same reasoning as above shows that b is the identity function.

(VI-12) Denjoy–Wolff Theorem. *Unless b is the identity function, it has a unique Denjoy-Wolff point.*

The uniqueness has just been shown. To establish the existence, assume that b has no fixed point in D. For $0 < r < 1$, let z_r be the fixed point of the function rb. As r tends to 1 the points z_r must tend to ∂D (for any cluster point in D would obviously be a fixed point of b). Hence, we can take a sequence of the points z_r, say $(z_n)_1^\infty$, that converges to a point z_0 in ∂D. Now

$$\|k_{z_r}^b\|_2^2 = \frac{1 - |b(z_r)|^2}{1 - |z_r|^2} = \frac{1 - |r^{-1} z_r|^2}{1 - |z_r|^2} \leq \frac{1}{r}.$$

Thus condition (C) holds with $c \leq 1$, and it follows by Carathéodory's theorem that b has an angular derivative in the sense of Carathéodory at z_0, with $|b'(z_0)| \leq 1$. Moreover, since $b(z_n)$ tends to z_0, the argument in the first step of the proof of Carathéodory's theorem (the argument showing condition (C) implies condition (VI-4)(ii)) shows that the function $\dfrac{1 - \overline{z}_0 b(z)}{1 - \overline{z}_0 z}$ is in $\mathcal{H}(b)$. Thus $b(z_0) = z_0$, so z_0 is the desired Denjoy–Wolff point.

(VI-13) Iteration. *Let z_0 be the Denjoy–Wolff point of b. For $n = 1, 2, \ldots$ let b_n be the n-th iterate of b ($b_1 = b$, $b_{n+1} = b \circ b_n$). Then, unless b is an elliptic Möbius transformation of D onto D, the sequence $(b_n)_1^\infty$ converges locally uniformly in D to the constant z_0.*

If z_0 lies in D then, assuming b is not an elliptic Möbius transformation, we have $|b'(z_0)| < 1$. Then in some disk centered at z_0 the inequality $|b(z)-z_0| < \frac{1}{2}(|b'(z_0)|+1)|z-z_0|$ holds, which implies that b_n tends to z_0 in that disk. That the convergence actually happens locally uniformly throughout D now follows by a standard result from the theory of normal families (Vitali's theorem).

Suppose z_0 is on ∂D. For $0 < r < 1$ let C_r denote the circle of radius r internally tangent to ∂D at z_0. If $b'(z_0) < 1$ then from Julia's lemma one sees that, for any r and any z in D, all but finitely many of the points $b_n(z)$ lie in the interior of C_r. Thus $b_n \to z_0$ pointwise, and by a slightly more careful application of Julia's lemma, or by an appeal to the theory of normal families, one sees that the convergence is locally uniform in D. It remains to consider the case where $b'(z_0) = 1$. That case breaks into two subcases, the one where equality holds in Julia's lemma and the one of strict inequality. In the former subcase b is a Möbius transformation that leaves each circle C_r invariant (a so-called parabolic Möbius transformation). Under a conformal map of D onto the upper half-plane that sends z_0 to ∞, such a b is transformed into a translation parallel to the real axis. The desired conclusion is clear in this case. In the other subcase, that where the inequality in Julia's lemma is strict, b sends each circle C_r (exclusive of the point z_0) into its interior. Consider a point z_{00} of D and its images $z_n = b_n(z_{00})$ ($n = 1, 2, \ldots$). For each n let r_n be the radius such that z_n lies on C_{r_n}. The numbers r_n then decrease as n increases. If the sequence (z_n) does not converge to z_0, then it has a subsequence (z_{n_k}) that converges to a point w distinct from z_0. The numbers r_n in this case have a positive limit r_0, and w lies on C_{r_0}. Thus $b(w)$ is in the interior of C_{r_0}. But $b(w)$ is the limit of z_{n_k+1} ($= b(z_{n_k})$), so z_{n_k+1} must eventually be in the interior of C_{r_0}. This is a contradiction because $r_n > r_0$ for all n. We can conclude that b_n converges pointwise to the constant z_0, and, as before, an appeal to the theory of normal families shows that the convergence is actually locally uniform.

Notes

(NVI-1) Julia's lemma in the form stated above, in (VI-6), is due to Carathéodory [16]. The original version of G. Julia [38, pp. 72ff.], [39] contained the hypothesis that b is regular at z_0, although Julia noted that that requirement can be somewhat relaxed. Carathéodory's proof, as well as Julia's, is based on Schwarz's lemma, of which Julia's lemma is an asymptotic variant.

(NVI-2) Carathéodory's original proof of his theorem [16] was based ultimately on Schwarz's lemma, as were proofs from the same time of R. Nevanlinna [50] and E. Landau and G. Valiron [40].

(NVI-3) The proof of Carathéodory's theorem presented here is adapted from the author's paper [61], much of which was inspired by earlier work of P. R. Ahern and D. N. Clark [2] pertaining to the case where b is an inner function. H. Dym independently had many of the same ideas as the author; they can be found in Chapter 8 of his monograph [24], where the setting is vector valued. The treatment here is an improvement of the one in [61] thanks to the incorporation of one of Dym's arguments, which is the main step in the proof that condition (IV-4)(ii) implies condition (IV-4)(iii). Dym, by the way, was unaware of Carathéodory's theorem at the time he did the work in question.

(NVI-4) The connection between angular derivatives and mass points goes back to Nevanlinna [49], the connection between angular derivatives and square integrability to M. Riesz [54].

(NVI-5) Ahern and Clark [3] have given a criterion for b to have an angular derivative at a given point of ∂D in terms of the zeros of b, the singular measure associated with the inner factor of b, and the measure $\frac{1}{2\pi} \log \frac{1}{|b|} d\theta$ on ∂D. The case where b is a Blaschke product goes back to O. Frostman [25].

(NVI-6) The designation "Denjoy–Wolff theorem" for (VI-12) is a slight misnomer, because it was the proposition (VI-13) on iteration that Denjoy and Wolff originally proved; this happened before Carathéodory's work on angular derivatives. Wolff [68] first established the result under the assumption that b extends continuously to $\overline{D}$ and slightly later [69] in the general case. In rapid succession Denjoy [21] found a second proof and Wolff [70] a third one. The proof above of (VI-12) follows a suggestion of de Branges.

(NVI-7) C. C. Cowen and Ch. Pommerenke [19] have obtained sharp inequalities involving derivatives at fixed points that give a quantative form to the uniqueness of the Denjoy–Wolff point. Proofs of their results using $\mathcal{H}(b)$ techniques have been obtained by K. Y. Li [42].

CHAPTER VII

HIGHER DERIVATIVES

A portion of the results on angular derivatives from the last chapter extend to higher derivatives. The results will be presented here, but the details of the proofs will be omitted.

(VII-1) Kernel Functions for Derivatives. For w a point of D and m a positive integer, the function $\partial^m k_w^b/\partial \overline{w}^m$ is easily seen to be the kernel function in $\mathcal{H}(b)$ for the functional of evaluation of the m-th derivative at w: for h in $\mathcal{H}(b)$, the inner product of h with this function equals $h^{(m)}(w)$. Since k_w^b is the image under the transformation V_b of the function $(1-\overline{b(w)})k_w$, the kernel function $\partial^m k_w^b/\partial \overline{w}^m$ is the image of the function $\partial^m[(1-\overline{b(w)})k_w]/\partial \overline{w}^m$. The analogous statement holds with μ_λ in place of μ, for each λ in ∂D.

(VII-2) Conditions for Nontangential Limits. *Let z_0 be a point of ∂D and let m be a nonnegative integer. The following conditions are equivalent.*

(i) *Each function in $\mathcal{H}(b)$ and all of its derivatives up to order m have nontangential limits at z_0.*

(ii) *The functions $\partial^m k_w^b/\partial \overline{w}^m$ stay bounded in the norm of $\mathcal{H}(b)$ as w tends radially to z_0.*

(iii) *There is a point λ in ∂D such that*

$$\int_{\partial D} |e^{i\theta} - z_0|^{-2m-2} d\mu_\lambda(e^{i\theta}) < \infty.$$

(iv) *The last inequality holds for all λ in $\partial D \setminus \{b(z_0)\}$.*

(v) *There is a point λ in ∂D such that μ_λ has a point mass at z_0 and*

$$\int_{\partial D \setminus \{z_0\}} |e^{i\theta} - z_0|^{-2m} d\mu_\lambda(e^{i\theta}) < \infty.$$

When these conditions hold, the function b and its derivatives up to order $m+1$ have nontangential limits at z_0.

(VII-3) Remarks on the Proof. The case $m = 0$ is contained in the results of Chapter VI. To establish the general case one assumes as an induction hypothesis that the theorem is true for $m - 1$.

The implication (i) $\Rightarrow$ (ii) of course follows from the principle of uniform boundedness, and the implication (iv) $\Rightarrow$ (iii) is trivial. The rest of the proof involves traveling between $\mathcal{H}(b)$ and the spaces $H^2(\mu_\lambda)$ with the aid of the transformations $V_{\overline{\lambda}b}$. All of the arguments are straightforward, but a few of them are a bit lengthy.

To show that (ii) implies (iv), one notes that (ii) says the rational functions $\partial^m[(1 - \lambda\overline{b(w)})k_w)]/\partial\overline{w}^m$ stay bounded in the norm of $H^2(\mu_\lambda)$ as w tends nontangentially to the point z_0. By Fatou's lemma, the limit function, obtained when one sets $w = z_0$, is in $L^2(\mu_\lambda)$. (The limit function exists pointwise because, by the induction hypothesis, b and its first m derivatives have nontangential limits at z_0.) Carrying out the differentiation using Leibniz's rule, one finds that, if $\lambda \neq b(z_0)$, the limit function has degree $m + 1$. Its only pole is at z_0, and the lower-order terms are in $L^2(\mu_\lambda)$ in virtue of the induction hypothesis. The leading term is thus also in $L^2(\mu_\lambda)$, which gives (iv). A similar argument, slightly more complicated, gives the implication (ii) $\Rightarrow$ (iv) (with $\lambda = b(1)$).

To prove that (iii) implies (i) one proves that (iii) implies the norm convergence of the functions $\overline{\partial}^m k_w^b/\partial\overline{w}^m$ as w tends nontangentially to z_0. To do that one examines the preimages of these functions under the transformation $V_{\overline{\lambda}b}$. The preimage of $\overline{\partial}^m k_w^b/\partial\overline{w}^m$ is a rational function of degree $m+1$ whose only pole is at $1/\overline{w}$ and whose coefficients involve $b(w), b'(w), \ldots, b^{(m)}(w)$, which by induction have nontangential limits at z_0. From that and condition (iii) one obtains the desired conclusion by a standard application of Fatou's lemma.

One closes the circle by showing that (v) implies (ii). Although this is the most complicated part of the proof, it involves the same basic ideas.

Finally, one shows, assuming the conditions hold, that $b^{(m+1)}$ has a nontangential limit at z_0 by using the existence of the nontangential limit at z_0 of the m-th derivative of the function $(b(z) - b(z_0))/(z - z_0)$. (As shown in Chapter VI, the latter function is in $\mathcal{H}(b)$.) The argument here also is a bit complicated but basically straightforward.

CHAPTER VIII

EQUALITY OF $\mathcal{H}(b)$ AND $\mathcal{H}(\bar{b})$

If $\mathcal{H}(b)$ and $\mathcal{H}(\bar{b})$ are equal as sets, then their norms are equivalent, by the closed graph theorem. An obvious case where that happens is the case $\|b\|_\infty < 1$, because then $\mathcal{H}(b)$ and $\mathcal{H}(\bar{b})$ are both renormed versions of H^2. An obvious case where it does not happen is the case where b is an inner function, because then $\mathcal{H}(\bar{b})$ is trivial. In this chapter the equality $\mathcal{H}(b) = \mathcal{H}(\bar{b})$ will be characterized in terms of b and in terms of the restricted backward shift operator. The situation is different depending upon whether b is extreme or nonextreme. In the nonextreme case, there is a connection with the corona theorem.

(VIII-1) Multiplier Characterization. *The equality* $\mathcal{H}(b) = \mathcal{H}(\bar{b})$ *holds if and only if b is a multiplier of $\mathcal{H}(b)$.*

This is a consequence of the equality $\mathcal{H}(b) \cap \mathcal{M}(b) = b\mathcal{H}(\bar{b})$ from (II-5). That equality implies that b multiplies $\mathcal{H}(\bar{b})$ into $\mathcal{H}(b)$. Hence, if $\mathcal{H}(b)$ and $\mathcal{H}(\bar{b})$ coincide, then b is a multiplier of $\mathcal{H}(b)$. In the other direction, if b is a multiplier of $\mathcal{H}(b)$, then the equality implies that $b\mathcal{H}(b) \subset b\mathcal{H}(\bar{b})$, so that $\mathcal{H}(b) \subset \mathcal{H}(\bar{b})$. Since the opposite inclusion is always true, one then has $\mathcal{H}(b) = \mathcal{H}(\bar{b})$.

(VIII-2) Invertibility and Equality of $\mathcal{H}(b)$ and $\mathcal{H}(\bar{b})$. *If b is invertible in H^∞ then $\mathcal{H}(b) = \mathcal{H}(\bar{b})$.*

To see this, assume b is invertible in H^∞, and write $\mathcal{H}(b) = T_{\bar{b}^{-1}} T_{\bar{b}} \mathcal{H}(b)$. Since $T_{\bar{b}} \mathcal{H}(b) \subset \mathcal{H}(\bar{b})$ by (II-4), and since $T_{\bar{b}^{-1}} \mathcal{H}(\bar{b}) \subset \mathcal{H}(\bar{b})$ by (II-7), it follows that $\mathcal{H}(b) \subset \mathcal{H}(\bar{b})$, and hence that $\mathcal{H}(b) = \mathcal{H}(\bar{b})$, as desired.

It will be shown shortly that the converse of the last proposition holds when b is extreme.

(VIII-3) Similarity of X. As shown in (III-2) and (III-3), the operator K_ρ is an isometry of $H^2(\rho)$ onto $\mathcal{H}(\bar{b})$, and it intertwines the operators Z_ρ^* (the adjoint of the operator on $H^2(\rho)$ of multiplication by the independent variable) and S^*. Thus, the restriction of S^* to $\mathcal{H}(\bar{b})$ is unitarily equivalent to Z_ρ^*. If $\mathcal{H}(b) = \mathcal{H}(\bar{b})$ then the norms of $\mathcal{H}(b)$ and $\mathcal{H}(\bar{b})$ are equivalent, so the operator $X \,(= S^*|\mathcal{H}(b))$ is similar to $S^*|\mathcal{H}(\bar{b})$ and hence also to Z_ρ^*. If b is extreme, then $H^2(\rho) = L^2(\rho)$, which means that Z_ρ is unitary. Hence, *if b is extreme and $\mathcal{H}(b) = \mathcal{H}(\bar{b})$, then the operator X is similar to a unitary operator.*

If b is nonextreme, then $\mathcal{H}(\bar{b}) = \mathcal{M}(\bar{a})$. The restriction of S^* to $\mathcal{M}(\bar{a})$ is unitarily equivalent to S^*, the unitary equivalence being implemented by $T_{\bar{a}}$. Hence, *if b is nonextreme and $\mathcal{H}(b) = \mathcal{H}(\bar{b})$, then the operator X is similar to S^*.*

(VIII-4) Identity for Difference Quotients. *If b is extreme then the equality $\|Xh\|_b^2 = \|h\|_b^2 - |h(0)|^2$ holds for all h in $\mathcal{H}(b)$.*

The equality will be used in establishing the converse of (VIII-2) for the case where b is extreme. Its proof will be based on the formula

$$X^*h = Sh - \langle h, S^*b\rangle_b b$$

from (II-9). From this formula we obtain, for h in $\mathcal{H}(b)$,

$$\begin{aligned}X^*Xh &= SS^*h - \langle Xh, S^*b\rangle_b b\\ &= h - h(0) - \langle Xh, S^*b\rangle_b b.\end{aligned}$$

If b is extreme then b is not in $\mathcal{H}(b)$ but $1 - \overline{b(0)}b \,(= k_0^b)$ is. The function $h(0) + \langle Xh, S^*b\rangle_b b$ appearing on the right side of the preceding equality, since it is in $\mathcal{H}(b)$, must then equal $h(0)k_0^b$, and we have $X^*Xh = h - h(0)k_0^b$, from which the desired equality, $\|Xh\|_b^2 = \|h\|_b^2 - |h(0)|^2$, is immediate.

(VIII-5) Characterization of the Equality $\mathcal{H}(b) = \mathcal{H}(\bar{b})$ for the Case Where b is Extreme. *If b is extreme, the following conditions are equivalent.*

(i) *b is invertible in H^∞.*
(ii) *$\mathcal{H}(b) = \mathcal{H}(\bar{b})$.*
(iii) *X is similar to a unitary operator.*

The implications (i) $\Rightarrow$ (ii) and (ii) $\Rightarrow$ (iii) are established above. To establish the implication (iii) $\Rightarrow$ (i) we assume that b is extreme but not invertible in H^∞. If X were similar to a unitary operator, or even to an isometry, there would be a positive constant c such that $\|X^nh\|_b \geq c\|h\|_b$

for all h in $\mathcal{H}(b)$ and all positive integers n. It will be shown that no such constant c exists.

Since b is not invertible in H^∞, the operator T_b is not invertible, and therefore neither is $T_{\bar b}$. But $T_{\bar b}$ has a dense range, so it must have 0 as an approximate eigenvalue. Hence, given any positive number ε, there is an f in H^2 with $\|f\|_2 = 1$ such that $\|T_{\bar b}f\|_2 < \varepsilon$. Let $h = (1 - T_b T_{\bar b})^{1/2} f$. Then h is in $\mathcal{H}(b)$, with $\|h\|_b \leq 1$, and

$$\|h\|_2^2 = \langle(1 - T_b T_{\bar b})f, f\rangle = \|f\|_2^2 - \|T_{\bar b}f\|_2^2$$
$$\geq 1 - \varepsilon^2.$$

From the preceding inequality we conclude that $\|h\|_b^2 \geq 1 - \varepsilon^2$. By iterating (VIII-4) we find that

$$\lim_{n\to\infty} \|X^n h\|_b^2 = \|h\|_b^2 - \|h\|_2^2.$$

The right side here is majorized by ε^2, because $\|h\|_b^2 \leq 1$ and $\|h\|_2^2 \geq 1 - \varepsilon^2$. This completes the proof.

(VIII-6) Corona Pairs. The functions g_1 and g_2 in H^∞ are said to form a corona pair if they satisfy the hypothesis of L. Carleson's corona theorem, that is, if $|g_1| + |g_2|$ is bounded away from 0 in D. When that happens, Carleson's theorem says that there are functions u_1 and u_2 in H^∞ such that $u_1 g_1 + u_2 g_2 = 1$.

(VIII-7) Characterization of the Equality $\mathcal{H}(b) = \mathcal{H}(\bar b)$ for the Case Where b is Nonextreme. Let b be nonextreme, and let the function a be defined as in Chapter IV. The following conditions are equivalent.
 (i) *The functions a and b form a corona pair.*
 (ii) $\mathcal{H}(b) = \mathcal{M}(\bar a)$.
 (iii) *X is similar to S^*.*

To prove that (i) implies (ii), assume a and b form a corona pair, and let u and v be H^∞ functions such that $ua + vb = 1$. Then, for h in $\mathcal{H}(b)$,

$$h = T_{\bar u} T_{\bar a} h + T_{\bar v} T_{\bar b} h = T_{\bar u} T_{\bar a} h + T_{\bar v} T_{\bar a} h^+$$
$$= T_{\bar a}(T_{\bar u} h + T_{\bar v} h^+),$$

proving that $\mathcal{H}(b) \subset \mathcal{M}(\bar a)$, and hence that $\mathcal{H}(b) = \mathcal{M}(\bar a)$.

To prove that (ii) implies (i), assume $\mathcal{H}(b) = \mathcal{M}(\bar{a})$. Then there is a positive constant c such that $\|h\|_{\bar{b}} \leq c\|h\|_b$ for all h in $\mathcal{H}(b)$. For w in D we have
$$\|k_w\|_b^2 = |a(w)|^{-2}(|a(w)|^2 + |b(w)|^2)(1 - |w|^2)^{-1}$$
by (IV-15). Since $T_{\bar{a}} k_w = \overline{a(w)} k_w$, we also have
$$\|k_w\|_{\bar{b}}^2 = |a(w)|^{-2}\|k_w\|_2^2 = |a(w)|^{-2}(1 - |w|^2)^{-1}.$$

Setting $h = k_w$ in the inequality above, we obtain $|a(w)|^2 + |b(w)|^2 \geq c^{-2}$, which proves a and b form a corona pair.

The implication (ii) $\Rightarrow$ (iii) is established above, in (VIII-3). To prove that (iii) implies (ii), assume S^* and X are similar, and let the operator A from H^2 onto $\mathcal{H}(b)$ implement the similarity. Then A can be regarded as a bounded operator on H^2 that commutes with S^*, so it equals $T_{\bar{u}}$ for some u in H^∞. Thus $\mathcal{H}(b) = \mathcal{M}(\bar{u})$. By Douglas's criterion (I-4), there is a positive constant c such that $T_{\bar{u}} T_u \leq c(1 - T_b T_{\bar{b}})$. Replacing u by a multiple of itself, if necessary, we can assume $c = 1$, so that $T_{\bar{u}} T_u \leq 1 - T_b T_{\bar{b}}$. As $T_u T_{\bar{u}} \leq T_{\bar{u}} T_u$, we then have $T_u T_{\bar{u}} + T_b T_{\bar{b}} \leq 1$. Hence, for w in D,
$$\|T_{\bar{u}} k_w\|_2^2 + \|T_{\bar{b}} k_w\|_2^2 \leq \|k_w\|_2^2,$$
in other words,
$$|u(w)|^2 \|k_w\|_2^2 + |b(w)|^2 \|k_w\|_2^2 \leq \|k_w\|_2^2.$$

Thus $|u|^2 + |b|^2 \leq 1$ in D and hence also on ∂D, implying $|u| \leq |a|$ on ∂D. Since a is an outer function, the function $v = u/a$ is therefore in H^∞, and we have the operator factorization $T_{\bar{u}} = T_{\bar{a}} T_{\bar{v}}$. Hence $\mathcal{M}(\bar{u}) \subset \mathcal{M}(\bar{a})$, and so also $\mathcal{H}(b) \subset \mathcal{M}(\bar{a})$, which implies that $\mathcal{H}(b) = \mathcal{M}(\bar{a})$, the desired conclusion.

Notes

(NVIII-1) The identity for difference quotients (VIII-4) goes back to de Branges and Rovnyak [14]. When b is nonextreme the equality $\|Xh\|_b^2 = \|h\|_b^2 - |h(0)|^2$ is replaced by the inequality $\|Xh\|_b^2 \leq \|h\|_b^2 - |h(0)|^2$. Details can be found in [14] and [58]. The treatment here is taken from the latter paper.

(NVIII-2) The characterization (VIII-5) is from the paper of Lotto and the author [44].

(NVIII-3) The characterization (VIII-7) is from the author's paper [59].

(NVIII-4) Lotto and the author prove in [44] that if b is extreme and is a multiplier of $\mathcal{H}(\bar{b})$, then b is invertible in H^∞, so that $\mathcal{H}(b) = \mathcal{H}(\bar{b})$.

(NVIII-5) The book of Garnett [27] is a good reference for the corona theorem. If b is nonextreme then, because of the way a is defined, $|a| + |b|$ is bounded away from 0 on ∂D. This suggests that a and b automatically form a corona pair when b is outer, but that is not the case, as one can see by means of a theorem of E. Lindelöf [27, p. 92]. Lindelöf's theorem says that if an H^∞ function has a one-sided limit at some point of ∂D, then it has the same radial limit at that point. Hence, if b is nonextreme and outer, and $|b|$ has one-sided limits of 0 and 1 at some point of ∂D, then a and b both have the radial limit 0 at that point and so do not form a corona pair.

(NVIII-6) The portions of propositions (VIII-5) and (VIII-7) pertaining to similarity of X illustrate a characterization of Sz.–Nagy and Foias [66] of Hilbert space contractions that are similar to isometries. Their result is that such a similarity holds if and only if the characteristic operator function of the given contraction is uniformly left invertible in the unit disk. If b is extreme, the characteristic operator function of the operator X^* is the scalar function b, and if b is nonextreme it is the two-by-one matrix function $\begin{pmatrix} b \\ a \end{pmatrix}$. Readers familiar with the Sz.–Nagy–Foias model theory will easily verify the preceding statements by examining the discussions in (IV-7) and (V-6).

A related result of Sz.–Nagy and Foias [65, p. 344] characterizes contractions similar to unitary operators and subsumes a portion of (VIII-5).

CHAPTER IX

EQUALITY OF $\mathcal{H}(b)$ AND $\mathcal{M}(a)$

In this chapter it is assumed that b is nonextreme. The functions F_λ ($|\lambda| = 1$) will be as defined in Chapter IV. We let Y denote the restriction operator $S|\mathcal{H}(b)$. (The S-invariance of $\mathcal{H}(b)$, when b is nonextreme, is established in (IV-5).) As shown in (IV-5), the spectrum of Y is $\overline{D}$.

The equality of the spaces $\mathcal{H}(b)$ and $\mathcal{M}(a)$ is related to a well-known theorem of H. Helson and G. Szegö. This chapter begins with some background on that theorem; references will be given in (NIX-1). Characterizations of the equality $\mathcal{H}(a) = \mathcal{M}(b)$ will be given in terms of Toeplitz operators, the functions a and b, the operator Y, and multipliers.

(IX-1) The Helson–Szegö Theorem. By a Helson–Szegö weight is meant a positive function on the unit circle of the form $\exp(x + \tilde{y})$, where x and y are real functions in L^∞, and $\|y\|_\infty < \pi/2$. (Here, $\tilde{y}$ denotes the conjugate function of y.) If ν is a positive measure on the unit circle then, according to the Helson–Szegö theorem, the projection P_+ is bounded on $L^2(\nu)$ if and only if ν is absolutely continuous and its Radon–Nikodym derivative is a Helson–Szegö weight.

(IX-2) Muckenhoupt's Condition (A_2). A positive function σ in L^1 is said to satisfy (A_2) if

$$\sup_I |I|^{-2} \int_I \sigma \, d\theta \int_I \sigma^{-1} d\theta < \infty;$$

here I ranges over all subarcs of ∂D. A theorem of R. Hunt, B. Muckenhoupt and R. Wheeden states that the projection P_+ is bounded on $L^2(\sigma)$ ($= L^2\left(\frac{1}{2\pi}\sigma d\theta\right)$) if and only if σ satisfies (A_2). Hence, σ is a Helson–Szegö weight if and only if it satisfies (A_2) (an equivalence for which a direct proof is lacking). (The Hunt–Muckenhoupt–Wheeden theorem is not used in any of the arguments to follow. It is mentioned by way of general background, because of its central role in the theory with which this chapter connects.)

(IX-3) Invertibility of Toeplitz Operators. Let f be an outer function in H^2. A theorem due (independently) to A. Devinatz and H. Widom tells us that the Toeplitz operator $T_{f/\bar{f}}$ is invertible if and only if $|f|^2$ is a Helson–Szegö weight. It should be noted that $T_{f/\bar{f}}$ always has a trivial kernel (so its invertibility is tantamount to its having full range). In fact, if $T_{f/\bar{f}} g = 0$, then $fg/\bar{f}$ is orthogonal to H^2, so $fg\ (= \bar{f}(fg/\bar{f}))$ is in both H^1 and $\overline{H}_0^1$ and is thus 0, implying that $g = 0$.

(IX-4) Characterization in Terms of Toeplitz Operators. *If there is a λ in ∂D such that the measure μ_λ is absolutely continuous and the operator $T_{F_\lambda/\overline{F}_\lambda}$ is invertible, then $\mathcal{H}(b) = \mathcal{M}(a)$. If $\mathcal{H}(b) = \mathcal{M}(a)$, then the preceding condition holds for every λ in ∂D.*

To prove this, fix a point λ in ∂D. As shown in (IV-13), the operator $T_{1-\bar{\lambda}b} T_{\overline{F}_\lambda}$ is an isometry of H^2 into $\mathcal{H}(b)$; its range is all of $\mathcal{H}(b)$ if and only if μ_λ is absolutely continuous. Consider the image under this operator of the range of the operator $T_{F_\lambda/\overline{F}_\lambda}$. One easily checks that $T_{\overline{F}_\lambda} T_{F_\lambda/\overline{F}_\lambda} = T_{F_\lambda}$, from which it is immediate that $T_{1-\bar{\lambda}b} T_{\overline{F}_\lambda} T_{F_\lambda/\overline{F}_\lambda} = T_a$. The image in question is thus $\mathcal{M}(a)$. It follows that $\mathcal{H}(b) = \mathcal{M}(a)$ if and only if μ_λ is absolutely continuous and $T_{F_\lambda/\overline{F}_\lambda}$ has full range. As noted above, in (IX-3), for $T_{F_\lambda/\overline{F}_\lambda}$ to be invertible it is sufficient that it have full range. This completes the proof.

(IX-5) Characterization in Terms of a and b. *For the equality $\mathcal{H}(b) = \mathcal{M}(a)$, it is necessary and sufficient that a and b form a corona pair and the operator $T_{a/\bar{a}}$ be invertible.*

The equality $T_{\bar{a}} T_{a/\bar{a}} = T_a$ implies that the equality $\mathcal{M}(\bar{a}) = \mathcal{M}(a)$ holds if and only if the operator $T_{a/\bar{a}}$ has full range, in other words, if and only if $T_{a/\bar{a}}$ is invertible. By (VIII-8), $\mathcal{H}(b) = \mathcal{M}(\bar{a})$ if and only if a and b form a corona pair. These two equivalences together yield the present characterization.

(IX-6) Characterization in Terms of Similarity. *For the equality $\mathcal{H}(b) = \mathcal{M}(a)$, it is necessary and sufficient that the operators Y and S be similar.*

The operator $S|\mathcal{M}(a)$ is unitarily equivalent to S, the equivalence being implemented by T_a. If $\mathcal{H}(b)$ and $\mathcal{M}(a)$ are equal then their norms are equivalent, by the closed graph theorem, implying that Y and S are similar.

For the other direction, assume that Y and S are similar, and let the operator A from H^2 onto $\mathcal{H}(b)$ implement the similarity. Then A is an operator on H^2 that commutes with S, so it equals T_u for some u in H^∞. The reasoning in the last part of the proof of (VIII-7) now carries over. Namely, the equality $\mathcal{H}(b) = \mathcal{M}(u)$ implies by Douglas's criterion (I-4) the inequality $T_u T_{\bar{u}} \leq c(1 - T_b T_{\bar{b}})$ for some positive constant c, which without loss of generality can be taken to be 1. It then follows as in (VIII-7) that the function u/a is in H^∞, implying the inclusion $\mathcal{M}(u) \subset \mathcal{M}(a)$ and hence the inclusion $\mathcal{H}(b) \subset \mathcal{M}(a)$. As the opposite inclusion is true always, we get the desired equality, $\mathcal{H}(b) = \mathcal{M}(a)$.

(IX-7) Commutant of Y. *The bounded operators on $\mathcal{H}(b)$ that commute with Y are the multiplication operators induced by the multipliers of $\mathcal{H}(b)$.*

It is obvious that the multiplication operators induced by multipliers commute with Y; their boundedness follows by the closed graph theorem (as noted in (II-10)). On the other hand, each point w of D is an eigenvalue of Y^* of unit multiplicity, the eigenspace being spanned by the kernel function $k_{\bar{w}}^b$. Hence each kernel function k_w^b is an eigenvector of M^* for any bounded operator M that commutes with Y. As shown in (II-10), that implies every such M is a multiplication operator.

(IX-8) Multiplier Characterization. *The equality $\mathcal{H}(b) = \mathcal{M}(a)$ holds if and only if every function in H^∞ is a multiplier of $\mathcal{H}(b)$.*

One direction is trivial, because every function in H^∞ is obviously a multiplier of $\mathcal{M}(a)$. To establish the other direction, assume every function in H^∞ is a multiplier of $\mathcal{H}(b)$. As in (II-10), we let M_φ denote the multiplication operator on $\mathcal{H}(b)$ induced by the multiplier φ. By (IX-7), the operator algebra $\{M_\varphi : \varphi \in H^\infty\}$ is a closed subalgebra of the algebra of all bounded operators on $\mathcal{H}(b)$. Thus, one can use the closed graph theorem to conclude that the map $\varphi \to M_\varphi$ is bounded, in other words, there is a positive constant c such that $\|M_\varphi\| \leq c\|\varphi\|_\infty$ for all φ in H^∞.

By (III-9), if φ is in H^∞, then the restriction of the Toeplitz operator $T_{\bar{\varphi}}$ to the disk algebra is a bounded operator on $L^2(\mu)$, with norm equal to $\|M_\varphi\|$ and so at most $c\|\varphi\|_\infty$. In particular, if n is any positive integer, and we denote the norm in $L^2(\mu)$ by $\|\cdot\|_\mu$, we have, for any (analytic) polynomial p,

$$\|S^{*n}p\|_\mu \leq c\|p\|_\mu, \qquad n = 1, 2, \ldots .$$

Let q be any trigonometric polynomial, and choose a positive integer n large enough so that the function $p(e^{i\theta}) = e^{in\theta}q(e^{i\theta})$ is an analytic polynomial. Then $P_+ q = S^{*n} p$, which in virtue of the inequality above implies that $\|P_+q\|_\mu \leq c\|q\|_\mu$. Hence P_+ is bounded on $L^2(\mu)$, and it follows by the Helson–Szegő theorem (IX-1) that μ is absolutely continuous and its Radon–Nikodym derivative is a Helson–Szegő weight. By (IX-3) and (IX-4), then, $\mathcal{H}(b) = \mathcal{M}(a)$, as desired.

Notes

(NIX-1) The book of Garnett [27] and the author's notes [57] contain material on the Helson–Szegö theorem and related matters. Both references contain proofs of the Helson–Szegö theorem. A proof of the Hunt–Muckenhoupt–Wheeden theorem appears in [27] and one of the invertibility criterion for Toeplitz operators in [57]. The book [26] of J. García–Cuervo and J. L. Rubio de Francia contains a wealth of information on weighted norm inequalities. Original sources are cited in all three of the volumes just mentioned.

(NIX-2) The characterizations (IX-5), (IX-6) and (IX-8) are from the author's paper [59]. The proofs here differ a bit from those in [59]. The connection between multipliers of $\mathcal{H}(b)$ and Helson–Szegö weights is given in the paper [20] of Davis and McCarthy.

(NIX-3) The two conditions entering into the characterization (IX-5), namely, that a and b form a corona pair and that $T_{a/\bar{a}}$ be invertible, are independent. In fact, when $b(z) = \dfrac{1+z}{2}$ (so $a(z) = \dfrac{1-z}{2}$), the functions a and b form a corona pair, yet $T_{a/\bar{a}}$ is not invertible. On the other hand, one can obtain an example in which $T_{a/\bar{a}}$ is invertible yet a and b do not form a corona pair by taking any b such that $T_{a/\bar{a}}$ is invertible but a is not invertible in H^∞, and then replacing b if necessary by its product with a suitable inner function. It is more difficult, however, to produce an example in which b is an outer function. One is given in [59]. In the construction there, one guarantees the invertibility of $T_{a/\bar{a}}$ by arranging to have $|a|^2$ satisfy (A_2).

(NIX-4) As noted in (NVIII-4), if b is extreme and is a multiplier of $\mathcal{H}(b)$, then $\mathcal{H}(b) = \mathcal{H}(\bar{b})$. This result does not carry over to the case where b is nonextreme. In fact, if b is nonextreme and $T_{a/\bar{a}}$ is invertible then, as pointed out in the proof of (IX-5), $\mathcal{M}(\bar{a}) = \mathcal{M}(a)$, so that every function in H^∞ is a multiplier of $\mathcal{M}(\bar{a})$. If in addition a and b fail to form a corona pair, then $\mathcal{H}(b) \neq \mathcal{M}(\bar{a})$, by (VIII-7).

CHAPTER X

NEAR EQUALITY OF $\mathcal{H}(b)$ AND $\mathcal{M}(a)$

We continue to assume that b is nonextreme. Conditions for $\mathcal{M}(a)$ to be dense in $\mathcal{H}(b)$, and for it to miss being dense by a finite-dimensional subspace, will be explored. The subject relates to a notion which arises in several other connections, that of a rigid function in H^1. Rigid functions are defined below and several of their basic properties derived; their structure is at present only partially understood. The main characterization of the density of $\mathcal{M}(a)$ in $\mathcal{H}(b)$ involves rigid functions and is useful in drawing certain conclusions about their structure.

Characterizations of when $\mathcal{M}(a)$ is of finite defect in $\mathcal{H}(b)$, and when it is closed and of finite defect, are given at the end of the chapter. As a preliminary, the boundary eigenvalues of the operator Y^* are investigated.

(X-1) Rigid Functions. A nonzero function in H^1 is called rigid if no other functions in H^1, except for positive scalar multiples of itself, have the same modulus as it almost everywhere on ∂D. Rigid functions are outer functions, for if u is a nonconstant inner function, then u and $(1+u)^2$ have the same argument on ∂D (so, if the H^1 function f is divisible by the inner function u, then it has the same argument on ∂D as $(1+u)^2 f/u$). Moreover, there are outer functions that are not rigid, for example, the function $(1+u)^2$, where u is a nonconstant inner function. More generally, if the H^1 function f is divisible in H^1 by $(1+u)^2$, then it is not rigid.

If the function f is in H^1 and $1/f$ is also in H^1, then f is rigid. In fact, if g is another function in H^1 with the same argument as f on ∂D, then g/f is in $H^{1/2}$ and is positive on ∂D, hence g/f is constant by a known theorem (referenced in (NX-1)). As will be shown shortly, the preceding sufficient condition for rigidity is not a necessary one.

(X-2) Rigid Functions and Toeplitz Operators. *If f is an outer function in H^2, then f^2 is rigid if and only if the operator $T_{\bar{f}/f}$ has a trivial kernel.*

To establish this, suppose first that the kernel of $T_{\overline{f}/f}$ contains the nonzero function g. The outer factor of g then also belongs to the kernel of $T_{\overline{f}/f}$, so we can assume without loss of generality that g is an outer function. The function $\overline{f}g/f$ is orthogonal to H^2, and it has the same modulus on ∂D as does g. It therefore equals $\overline{u g}$ where u is an inner function that vanishes at the origin. We thus have $f/\overline{f} = ug/\overline{g}$, in other words, the function ug^2 has the same argument on ∂D as does f^2, showing that f^2 is not rigid.

Suppose, conversely, that f^2 is not rigid, in other words, that there is a function in H^1, not a positive scalar multiple of f^2, whose argument agrees with that of f^2 on ∂D. There is then an outer function with the preceding properties. In fact, if the original function happens to have the inner factor u, we can replace u by either $(1+u)^2$ or $-(1-u)^2$; that yields two outer functions with the same argument on ∂D as f^2, and at most one of them is a constant multiple of f^2. Thus, there is an outer function g in H^2, not a constant multiple of f, such that f^2 and g^2 have the same argument on ∂D. The function $\overline{f(0)}g - \overline{g(0)}f$ is then nonzero, and, because $\overline{f}/f = \overline{g}/g$, one easily verifies that it belongs to the kernel of $T_{\overline{f}/f}$.

(X-3) An Example. An example is now at hand of a rigid function whose reciprocal is not in H^1. The example is the function $z + 1$. Its argument on ∂D is $\theta/2$ $(-\pi < \theta < \pi)$. If it were not rigid then, by (X-2), the Toeplitz operator with symbol $e^{-i\theta/2}$ would have a nontrivial kernel. Let the function g be in the kernel of that operator. Then the function $e^{i\theta/2}\overline{g}$ is in H^2 and it vanishes at the origin, so $e^{i\theta}\overline{g}^2$ is H^1 and it has at least a double zero at the origin. Since g^2 is in H^1, that can only happen if $g = 0$, the desired conclusion.

(X-4) Rigidity and Density of $\mathcal{M}(a)$. *If there is a point λ in ∂D such that the measure μ_λ is absolutely continuous and the function F_λ^2 is rigid, then $\mathcal{M}(a)$ is dense in $\mathcal{H}(b)$. If $\mathcal{M}(a)$ is dense in $\mathcal{H}(b)$, then the preceding condition holds for every point λ in ∂D.*

The proof is similar to the proof of (IX-4). Fix a point λ on ∂D. As in (IX-4), the operator $T_{1-\overline{\lambda}b}T_{\overline{F}_\lambda}$ is an isometry of H^2 into $\mathcal{H}(b)$; its range is all of $\mathcal{H}(b)$ if and only if μ_λ is absolutely continuous. The image under this isometry of the range of the operator $T_{F_\lambda/\overline{F}_\lambda}$ is $\mathcal{M}(a)$, which is therefore dense in $\mathcal{H}(b)$ if and only if μ_λ is absolutely continuous and the range of $T_{F_\lambda/\overline{F}_\lambda}$ is dense in H^2. The latter condition holds if and only if the kernel of $T_{\overline{F}_\lambda/F_\lambda}$ is trivial, in other words, by (X-2), if and only if F_λ^2 is rigid.

(X-5) Rigidity and Closeness to Zero. *Let f and f_1 be outer functions in H^2 such that f_1^2 is rigid and $|f| \geq |f_1|$. Then f^2 is rigid.*

In fact, if f^2 is not rigid then, by (X-2), there is a nonzero function g in the kernel of $T_{\bar{f}/f}$. The function gf_1/f is then in H^2 and, as one easily verifies, is annihilated by $T_{\bar{f}_1/f_1}$, implying, again by (X-2), that f_1^2 is not rigid. (One can also deduce the result directly from the definition of rigidity.)

Whether an outer function in H^1 is rigid thus depends, in some sense, on how close the function is to 0.

(X-6) Sufficient Condition for Density of $\mathcal{M}(a)$. *If the function a^2 is rigid, then $\mathcal{M}(a)$ is dense in $\mathcal{H}(b)$.*

In fact, if a^2 is rigid then, by (X-5), so is F_λ^2 for every λ. That implies by (X-4) and (IV-10) that $\mathcal{M}(a)$ is dense in $\mathcal{H}(b)$.

The rigidity of a^2 is not a necessary condition for the density of $\mathcal{M}(a)$ in $\mathcal{H}(b)$, however. Further details are given in (NX-4).

(X-7) Quasisimilarity. Two operators T_1 and T_2, acting on the respective Hilbert spaces H_1 and H_2, are said to be quasisimilar if there is a quasiaffinity A from H_1 to H_2 such that $AT_1 = T_2A$ and a quasiaffinity B from H_2 to H_1 such that $T_1B = BT_2$. A quasiaffinity is by definition a one-to-one operator with a dense range.

(X-8) Density of $\mathcal{M}(a)$ and Quasisimilarity. *The operators Y and S are quasisimilar if and only if $\mathcal{M}(a)$ is dense in $\mathcal{H}(b)$.*

If $\mathcal{M}(a)$ is dense in $\mathcal{H}(b)$, then T_a, regarded as an operator from H^2 into $\mathcal{H}(b)$, is one of the required quasiaffinities intertwining S and Y, and the injection of $\mathcal{H}(b)$ into H^2 is the other one.

Suppose on the other hand that A is a quasiaffinity from H^2 to $\mathcal{H}(b)$ such that $AS = YA$. Then A is also an operator on H^2 that commutes with S, so it equals T_u for some function u in H^∞. The reasoning in (IX-6) now applies to show that the range of T_u is contained in the range of T_a, implying that $\mathcal{M}(a)$ is dense in $\mathcal{H}(b)$.

(X-9) Exposed Points. In a real or complex vector space, a point p of a convex set is called an exposed point of the set if there is a real linear functional on the space that attains its maximum over the set at the point p and only there. An exposed point is thus always an extreme point. A simple example of a closed convex set that possesses nonexposed extreme points is a closed square in the plane surmounted by a closed half-disk, the diameter of the half-disk being the same as the side-length of the square. The two extremities of the segment where the square and half-disk meet are extreme points but not exposed points.

It is known that the extreme points of the unit ball in the space H^1 are the outer functions of unit norm. (The reference is noted in (NX-3).)

(X-10) Rigidity and Exposed Points. *Let f be a function of unit norm in H^1. Then f is an exposed point of the unit ball if and only if f is a rigid function.*

This is nearly a tautology. First of all, one easily verifies that f is an exposed point of the unit ball of H^1 if and only if there is a linear functional on H^1 of unit norm that takes the value 1 at f but at no other point of the unit ball. By the Hahn–Banach theorem, a linear functional on H^1 of unit norm is induced by an L^∞ function of unit norm. The only such functional that takes the value 1 at f is the one induced by the function $|f|/f$. The only functions in the unit ball of H^1 at which the latter functional takes the value 1 are those having the same argument as f on ∂D. The desired conclusion is now immediate.

(X-11) Structure of Rigid Functions. At present there is no simple structural characterization of rigid functions. The problem of characterizing rigidity will be discussed further in the Notes at the end of the chapter. The Notes also mention a few additional contexts in which rigidity arises.

We proceed to an investigation of the circumstances under which the closure of $\mathcal{M}(a)$ has a finite codimension in $\mathcal{H}(b)$.

(X-12) An Intertwining. *Let λ be a point of ∂D such that the measure μ_λ is absolutely continuous. Then the operator $T_{1-\bar\lambda b}T_{\overline{F}_\lambda}$ intertwines the operator $S^* - F_\lambda(0)^{-1}(S^*F_\lambda \otimes 1)$ on H^2 with the operator Y^* on $\mathcal{H}(b)$.*

Let A_λ denote the operator on H^2 that $T_{1-\bar\lambda b}T_{\overline{F}_\lambda}$ transforms into Y^*. From the relation between the operator $T_{1-\bar\lambda b}T_{\overline{F}_\lambda}$ and the operator $V_{\bar\lambda b}$, given in (IV-13), one sees that, for w in D, the image under $T_{1-\bar\lambda b}T_{\overline{F}_\lambda}$ of the function $F_\lambda k_w$ is the image under $V_{\bar\lambda b}$ of the function k_w, which by (III-7) is the function $(1 - \lambda\overline{b(w)})^{-1}k_w^b$. The operator Y^* has k_w^b as an eigenvector, with eigenvalue $\bar w$. Hence $A_\lambda F_\lambda k_w = \bar w F_\lambda k_w$. This family of equalities uniquely determines A_λ, because, F_λ being an outer function, the functions $F_\lambda k_w$ ($|w| < 1$) span H^2.

Since
$$S^* F_\lambda k_w = F_\lambda S^* k_w + k_w(0) S^* F_\lambda$$
$$= \overline{w} F_\lambda k_w + S^* F_\lambda,$$
we have
$$S^* F_\lambda k_w - A_\lambda F_\lambda k_w = S^* F_\lambda.$$
Thus, the difference $S^* - A_\lambda$ is an operator of rank 1 whose range is spanned by the function $S^* F_\lambda$:
$$S^* - A_\lambda = (S^* F_\lambda) \otimes v,$$
where v is the function in H^2 that satisfies $\langle F_\lambda k_w, v \rangle = 1$ for all w. Since all the functions $F_\lambda k_w$ take the same value, $F_\lambda(0)$, at the origin, v is in fact the constant function $1/\overline{F_\lambda(0)}$, and we have the desired equality:
$$A_\lambda = S^* - F_\lambda(0)^{-1}(S^* F_\lambda \otimes 1).$$

(X-13) Boundary Eigenvalues of Y^*. *Let z_0 be a point of ∂D and λ a point of ∂D such that the measure μ_λ is absolutely continuous. The following conditions are equivalent*

(i) $\overline{z}_0$ *is an eigenvalue of* Y^*.
(ii) *The function* $F_\lambda(z)/(1 - \overline{z}_0 z)$ *is in* H^2.
(iii) *The function b has an angular derivative in the sense of Carathéodory at* z_0.

The equivalence of (ii) and (iii) is given by (VI-8) and (VI-9). To prove that (i) and (ii) are equivalent it will suffice, because of (X-12), to prove that (ii) holds if and only if $\overline{z}_0$ is an eigenvalue of the operator
$$A_\lambda = S^* - F_\lambda(0)^{-1}(S^* F_\lambda \otimes 1).$$
Suppose the H^2 function g lies in the kernel of $A_\lambda - \overline{z}_0$:
$$\overline{z}_0 g = S^* g - F_\lambda(0)^{-1} g(0) S^* F_\lambda.$$
Applying the operator S to both sides of the preceding equality, we obtain
$$\overline{z}_0 S g = g - g(0) - F_\lambda(0)^{-1} g(0)(F_\lambda - F_\lambda(0))$$
$$= g - F_\lambda(0)^{-1} g(0) F_\lambda,$$

in other words,
$$(1 - \bar{z}_0 z)g = g(0)F_\lambda(0)^{-1}F_\lambda.$$

If g is not the zero function we conclude from the last equality that (ii) holds. Conversely, if (ii) holds we see from the preceding calculations that $\bar{z}_0$ is an eigenvalue of A_λ, the eigenspace being one dimensional and spanned by the function $F_\lambda/(1 - \bar{z}_0 z)$.

(X-14) Root Subspaces. *Let z_0 be a point of ∂D and λ a point of ∂D such that the measure μ_λ is absolutely continuous. Assume that there is a largest positive integer m such that the function $F_\lambda(z)/(1-\bar{z}_0 z)^m$ lies in H^2. Then the kernel of the operator $(Y^* - \bar{z}_0)^k$ has dimension k for $k \leq m$ and dimension m for $k \geq m$.*

Because of (X-12), it will suffice to prove the analogous statement for the operator A_λ. It will be shown that the kernel of $(A_\lambda - \bar{z}_0)^k$ is spanned by the functions $(1 - \bar{z}_0 z)^{-1}F_\lambda, \ldots, (1 - \bar{z}_0 z)^{-k}F_\lambda$ for $k \leq m$ and by the functions $(1 - \bar{z}_0 z)^{-1}F_\lambda, \ldots, (1 - \bar{z}_0 z)^{-m}F_\lambda$ for $k \geq m$. The case $k = 1$ is established by (X-13) and its proof, so we can proceed by induction, assuming as an induction hypothesis that the desired conclusion holds for $k - 1$.

Suppose first that the function g lies in the kernel of $(A_\lambda - \bar{z}_0)^k$. Let j be the minimum of $k - 1$ and m. Then, by the induction hypothesis, $(A_\lambda - \bar{z}_0)g$, being in the kernel of $(A_\lambda - \bar{z}_0)^{k-1}$, equals $(1 - \bar{z}_0 z)^{-j}pF_\lambda$ for some polynomial p of degree at most $j - 1$. Since

$$(A_\lambda - \bar{z}_0)g = S^*g - F_\lambda(0)^{-1}g(0)S^*F_\lambda - \bar{z}_0 g$$
$$= \frac{g - g(0)}{z} - F_\lambda(0)^{-1}g(0)\left(\frac{F_\lambda - F_\lambda(0)}{z}\right) - \bar{z}_0 g$$
$$= z^{-1}[(1 - \bar{z}_0 z)g - F_\lambda(0)^{-1}g(0)F_\lambda],$$

we can conclude that $g = (1 - \bar{z}_0 z)^{-j-1}qF_\lambda$, where

$$q = zp + F_\lambda(0)^{-1}g(0)(1 - \bar{z}_0 z)^j,$$

a polynomial of degree at most j. In case $k > m$ (i.e., $j = m$), the function $(1 - \bar{z}_0 z)^{-j-1}qF_\lambda$ is not in H^2 unless $q(z_0) = 0$, in which case it can be rewritten as $(1 - \bar{z}_0 z)^{-j}q_1 F_\lambda$ where q_1 is a polynomial of degree at most $j - 1$. Thus, in case $k \leq m$ the function g lies in the span of the functions $(1 - \bar{z}_0 z)^{-1}F_\lambda, \ldots, (1 - \bar{z}_0 z)^{-k}F_\lambda$, and in case $k > m$ it lies in the span of the functions $(1 - \bar{z}_0 z)^{-1}F_\lambda, \ldots, (1 - \bar{z}_0 z)^{-m}F_\lambda$, as desired.

To complete the proof it will suffice, by the induction hypothesis, to prove that, in case $1 < k \leq m$, the function $(A_\lambda - \overline{z}_0)[(1-\overline{z}_0 z)^{-k} F_\lambda]$ is of the form $(1-\overline{z}_0 z)^{-k+1} pF_\lambda$, where p is a polynomial of degree at most $k-2$. This is true with $p = z^{-1}[1-(1-\overline{z}_0 z)^{k-1}]$, as one sees by setting $g = (1-\overline{z}_0 z)^{-k} F_\lambda$ in the expression above for $(A_\lambda - \overline{z}_0)g$.

The preceding proof shows, incidentally, that if $(1-\overline{z}_0 z)^{-k} F_\lambda$ is in H^2 for all positive integers k, then the kernel of $(Y^* - \overline{z}_0)^k$ has dimension k for all k.

(X-15) The Space $\mathcal{H}_0(b)$. In case $\mathcal{M}(a)$ is not dense in $\mathcal{H}(b)$, we let $\mathcal{H}_0(b)$ denote the orthogonal complement of $\mathcal{M}(a)$ in $\mathcal{H}(b)$. The orthogonal projection in $\mathcal{H}(b)$ with range $\mathcal{H}_0(b)$ will be denoted by P_0, and the compression of the operator Y to $\mathcal{H}_0(b)$ will be denoted by $Y_0 : Y_0 = P_0 Y|\mathcal{H}_0(b)$. (Thus, Y_0^* is the restriction of Y^* to $\mathcal{H}_0(b)$.)

If z_0 is a point of ∂D and k is a positive integer, then any function in the kernel of $(Y^* - \overline{z}_0)^k$ lies in $\mathcal{H}_0(b)$ and so is actually in the kernel of $(Y_0^* - \overline{z}_0)^k$. For such a function is orthogonal to $(Y - z_0)^k \mathcal{H}(b)$, and hence to $(Y - z_0)^k \mathcal{M}(a)$. But $Y|\mathcal{M}(a)$ is unitarily equivalent to S (the equivalence being implemented by T_a), so $(Y - z_0)^k \mathcal{M}(a)$ is dense in $\mathcal{M}(a)$ relative to the norm of $\mathcal{M}(a)$ and so also relative to the norm of $\mathcal{H}(b)$.

We note that if φ is a multiplier of $\mathcal{H}(b)$ then, because $\mathcal{M}(a)$ is invariant under the operator M_φ (= $T_\varphi|\mathcal{H}(b)$), the space $\mathcal{H}_0(b)$ is invariant under M_φ^*. From this one sees that if φ and ψ are two multipliers of $\mathcal{H}(b)$, then $P_0 M_\varphi P_0 M_\psi P_0 = P_0 M_{\varphi\psi} P_0$.

(X-16) Spectrum of Y_0. *If $\mathcal{M}(a) \neq \mathcal{H}(b)$, then the spectrum of the operator Y_0 is contained in the unit circle.*

As noted earlier, in (IV-6), the spectrum of the operator Y is $\overline{D}$, and if $|w| > 1$, then the inverse of $Y - w$ is the multiplication operator M_φ induced by the function $\varphi(z) = (z-w)^{-1}$. By the remark at the end of (X-15), the operator $P_0 M_\varphi|\mathcal{H}_0(b)$ then inverts to operator $Y_0 - w$. Thus, the spectrum of Y_0 is contained in $\overline{D}$.

If $|w| < 1$, then the function $\varphi(z) = a(w)^{-1}(z-w)^{-1}(a(w) - a(z))$ (= $-a(w)^{-1}(Q_w a)(z)$) is a multiplier of $\mathcal{H}(b)$, since a is (see (II-10)). By the remark at the end of (X-15), again, the operator $P_0 M_\varphi|\mathcal{H}_0(b)$ inverts $Y_0 - w$. Thus, the spectrum of Y_0 is disjoint from D.

(X-17) Condition for $\mathcal{M}(a)$ to Have a Finite Defect. *Let N be a* positive integer, and let λ be a point of ∂D such that the measure μ_λ is absolutely continuous. The following conditions are equivalent.

(i) The codimension of $\overline{\mathcal{M}(a)}$ in $\mathcal{H}(b)$ is N.

(ii) $F_\lambda = pf$, where p is a polynomial of degree N having all of its roots on the unit circle, and f is a function in H^2 whose square is rigid.

Of course, because the isometry $T_{1-\bar\lambda b}T_{\bar F_\lambda}$ of H^2 onto $\mathcal{H}(b)$ maps the range of the operator $T_{F_\lambda/\bar F_\lambda}$ onto $\mathcal{M}(a)$, condition (i) holds if and only if the dimension of the kernel of $T_{\bar F_\lambda/F_\lambda}$ is N.

Assume (i) holds. By (X-16), the spectrum of the operator Y_0 lies on the unit circle. Let $z_1,\ldots,z_s$ be the eigenvalues of Y_0 and $m_1,\ldots,m_s$ their algebraic multiplicities (the dimensions of the corresponding root subspaces). The sum $m_1 + \cdots + m_s$ is then the dimension of $\mathcal{H}_0(b)$, in other words, N. The structure of the operator Y_0^* is determined by (X-14): the kernel of $(Y_0^* - \bar z_j)^k$ has dimension k for $k \leq m_j$ and dimension m_j for $k \geq m_j$. Let $p(z) = (1 - \bar z_1 z)^{m_1}\ldots(1 - \bar z_s z)^{m_s}$, a polynomial of degree N. By (X-14), the function $f = F_\lambda/p$ belongs to H^2. It remains, in order to establish (ii), to prove that f^2 is rigid, or, equivalently, that the operator $T_{\bar f/f}$ has a trivial kernel. One easily sees that $p/\bar p$ is a unimodular constant times z^N, so that $T_{\bar f/f}$ is a unimodular constant times $T_{\bar F_\lambda/F_\lambda}S^N$. It is thus enough to show that the kernel of $T_{\bar F_\lambda/F_\lambda}$ has a trivial intersection with $S^N H^2$. If that intersection contained a nonzero function g, then the linearly independent functions $g, S^*g, \ldots, S^{*N}g$ would all belong to the kernel of $T_{\bar F_\lambda/F_\lambda}$, a contradiction, since the kernel has dimension N. Thus the kernel of $T_{\bar f/f}$ is trivial, and the implication (i) $\Rightarrow$ (ii) is established.

Assume, conversely, that (ii) holds. As above, the function $\bar p/p$ is a constant multiple of $\bar z^N$, from which it follows that $T_{\bar F_\lambda/F_\lambda}$ is a constant multiple of $S^{*N}T_{\bar f/f}$. The kernel of S^{*N} consists of the polynomials of degrees less than N. The kernel of $T_{\bar F_\lambda/F_\lambda}$ thus consists of all functions mapped by $T_{\bar f/f}$ to polynomials of degrees less than N. The space of such functions has dimension at most N, since $T_{\bar f/f}$ has a trivial kernel. But if q is a polynomial then the image of qf under $T_{\bar f/f}$ is a polynomial of the same degree, so in fact the kernel of $T_{\bar F_\lambda/F_\lambda}$ is of dimension N, in other words, (i) holds.

(X-18) Condition for $\mathcal{M}(a)$ to be Closed and of Finite Defect. *Let N be a positive integer, and let λ be a point of ∂D such that the measure μ_λ is absolutely continuous. The following conditions are equivalent.*

(i) *$\mathcal{M}(a)$ is closed in $\mathcal{H}(b)$, and its codimension is N.*

(ii) $F_\lambda = pf$, where p is a polynomial of degree N having all of its roots on the unit circle, and f is an outer function in H^2 such that $|f|^2$ is a Helson–Szegö weight.

In view of the correspondence between H^2 and $\mathcal{H}(b)$ produced by the operator $T_{1-\bar{\lambda}b}T_{\overline{F}_\lambda}$, condition (i) holds if and only if the operator $T_{F_\lambda/\overline{F}_\lambda}$ has a closed range of codimension N. And because, as mentioned in (IX-3), the operator $T_{F_\lambda/\overline{F}_\lambda}$ always has a trivial kernel, the latter condition holds if and only if $T_{F_\lambda/\overline{F}_\lambda}$ is a Fredholm operator of index $-N$.

The implication (i) $\Rightarrow$ (ii) is a small variation of the corresponding implication in (X-17). Namely, if (i) holds then, by (X-17), we have $F_\lambda = pf$, where p is a polynomial of the required form, and f is an outer function in H^2. As in the proof of (X-17), the operator $T_{f/\bar{f}}$ is a constant multiple of $S^{*N}T_{F_\lambda/\overline{F}_\lambda}$. Since S^{*N} is Fredholm of index N and $T_{F_\lambda/\overline{F}_\lambda}$, because of (i), is Fredholm of index $-N$, the operator $T_{f/\bar{f}}$ is Fredholm of index 0, hence invertible. As noted in (IX-3), that implies $|f|^2$ is a Helson–Szegö weight, so (ii) holds.

Conversely, if (ii) holds, then we can reverse the preceding reasoning to conclude that the operator $T_{F_\lambda/\overline{F}_\lambda}$ is Fredholm of index $-N$, so that (i) holds.

Notes

(NX-1) The result that a function in $H^{1/2}$ is constant if it is positive almost everywhere on ∂D is in a paper of J. Neuwirth and D. J. Newman [48], and implicitly in a paper of H. Helson and the author [34].

(NX-2) Rigid functions arise in a problem in prediction theory, namely, the problem of characterizing the spectral densities of completely nondeterministic Gaussian sequences. That connection, along with the characterizations in terms of Toeplitz operators and exposed points given in (X-2) and (X-10), can be found in a paper of P. Bloomfield, N. P. Jewell and E. Hayashi [11]. The example (X-3) is in the same paper. More generally, K. Yabuta [71], [72] has shown that a polynomial without zeros in D and without multiple zeros on ∂D is a rigid function.

(NX-3) The result that the extreme points of the unit ball of H^1 are the outer functions of unit norm is due to K. de Leeuw and W. Rudin [41]. That paper is the starting point of the developments that occupy this chapter.

(NX-4) The connection between rigidity and the density of $\mathcal{M}(a)$ in $\mathcal{H}(b)$ is pointed out in the author's paper [62]. That paper also contains an example in which $\mathcal{M}(a)$ is dense in $\mathcal{H}(b)$ yet a^2 is not rigid, showing that the converse of (X-6) fails. In the example, a is the function $\dfrac{1+z}{2}$.

(NX-5) If $\mathcal{M}(a)$ is dense in $\mathcal{H}(b)$ and u is an inner function, then $\mathcal{M}(a)$ is dense in $\mathcal{H}(ub)$. In fact, the inequality $1 - T_b T_{\bar{b}} \leq 1 - T_{ub} T_{\overline{ub}}$ implies that $\mathcal{H}(b)$ is contained contractively in $\mathcal{H}(ub)$, and it is dense in $\mathcal{H}(ub)$ because it contains the polynomials. The desired conclusion is now clear. Thus, by (X-4), if $\mathcal{M}(a)$ is dense in $\mathcal{H}(b)$, then not only is $a^2/(1-\bar{\lambda}b)^2$ $(= F_\lambda^2)$ rigid for all unimodular constants λ, but $a^2/(1-ub)^2$ is rigid for all inner functions u. (This result, with a somewhat more circuitous proof, is in [62].) However, the example mentioned at the end of (NX-4) shows that the density of $\mathcal{M}(a)$ in $\mathcal{H}(ub)$ for an inner function u does not imply the density of $\mathcal{M}(a)$ in $\mathcal{H}(b)$.

(NX-6) Rigid functions in H^1 and related topics have been explored by a number of authors. Besides the papers already mentioned, there are others by E. Hayashi [30], [31], H. Helson [32], [33], T. Nakazi [45], [46], [47], J. Inoue and Nakazi [36], R. Younis [73], K. Izuchi and Younis [37], and the author [63]. However, as noted in (X-11), we still lack a structural characterization of rigidity.

In [62] the author advanced a conjecture about the structure of rigid functions. Let f be an outer function in H^2. Suppose b is a function in the unit ball of H^∞ such that $\dfrac{1-|b|^2}{|1-b|^2}$ is the Poisson integral of $|f|^2$. Thus, $f = F_1$. The conjecture states that the following three conditions are equivalent:

(i) f^2 is rigid.

(ii) There is no nonconstant inner function u such that $f/(1-u)$ is in H^2.

(iii) μ_λ is absolutely continuous for every λ in ∂D.

The implication (i) $\Rightarrow$ (ii) is simple, as explained in (X-1). The implication (i) $\Rightarrow$ (iii), which was established in [62], is contained in (X-4), and the implication (ii) $\Rightarrow$ (iii), established in [63], is contained in (IV-17). In [63] a portion of the implication (iii) $\Rightarrow$ (i) is established, and in [S10] the implication (ii) $\Rightarrow$ (i) is shown to hold in certain cases. However, J. Inoue [S5] has recently constructed an example showing that the implication (ii) $\Rightarrow$ (i) fails in general, thus refuting the conjecture. I am uncertain about the status of the implication (iii) $\Rightarrow$ (ii). V. Kapustin has reported having a counterexample, but I have not seen the details.

(NX-7) Proposition (X-17) gives an alternative approach to a prediction-theoretic result due independently to Bloomfield, Jewell and Hayashi [11, Theorem 11] and Nakazi [47, Theorem 9]. Proposition (X-18) gives an alternative approach to a prediction-theoretic result of Helson and the author [34, Theorem 6].

CHAPTER XI

BRIEF MENTION OF A FEW ADDITIONAL TOPICS

(XI-1) Nehari Problem. The Nehari interpolation problem asks for the functions in the unit ball of L^∞ having a prescribed sequence of negatively indexed Fourier coefficients. A linear fractional parameterization of the solution set in the indeterminate case has been obtained by V. M. Adamyan, D. Z. Arov and M. G. Krein [1] and derived in another way by J. B. Garnett [27]. The ingredients involved are among those one encounters when exploring $\mathcal{H}(b)$ for the case where b is not an extreme point. In particular, as was pointed out in [62], a solution to the problem of characterizing the rigid functions in H^1 would at the same time answer a natural question about the Nehari problem. The author believes that the connection between the spaces $\mathcal{H}(b)$ and the Nehari problem has yet to be fully revealed.

(XI-2) Kernels of Toeplitz Operators. This is another topic in which rigid functions in H^1 make an appearance. The story begins with a theorem of D. Hitt [S4] which characterizes the nearly invariant subspaces of the backward shift operator, S^*, on H^2. A subspace M of H^2 is called nearly S^*-invariant if S^*h is in M whenever h is in M and $h(0) = 0$. Hitt's theorem states that any such M is of the form $M = T_g M'$, where the function g is in H^2 and of unit norm, the subspace M' is S^*-invariant, and the operator T_g acts as an isometry on M'.

If the subspace M' in Hitt's theorem is all of H^2, then the only way that T_g can act isometrically on it is for g to be an inner function. If the subspace M' is proper, on the other hand, it equals $\mathcal{H}(u)$ for some inner function u, which turns out to vanish at the origin. The question now arises how g and u must be related in order for T_g to act isometrically on $\mathcal{H}(u)$.

In [60] the author presented an approach to Hitt's theorem, based on de Branges-Rovnyak spaces, which clarifies the last point. Suppose the subspace M' in Hitt's theorem equals $\mathcal{H}(u)$ for an inner function u. Let b be the function in the unit ball of H^∞ such that $b(0) = 0$ and the real part of $\dfrac{1+b}{1-b}$ is the Poisson integral of $|g|^2$. (The choice $b(0) = 0$ is possible because $|g|^2$ has unit norm in L^1.) The result from [60] is that the inner function u must divide the inner factor of the function b.

Independently of Hitt, E. Hayashi [30], [31] studied the kernels of Toeplitz operators on H^2. If M is the kernel of a nontrivial Toeplitz operator then M is nearly S^*-invariant, so Hitt's theorem applies. As a corollary to Hitt's theorem one sees that M has the form $M = T_g\mathcal{H}(u)$, where the function u is inner with $u(0) = 0$, the function g is outer with unit norm in H^2, and the operator T_g acts isometrically on $\mathcal{H}(u)$. Hayashi obtained these conclusions by different reasoning, and he showed that, in addition, the function g^2 must be rigid.

The question now arises whether the preceding description of the kernels of Toeplitz operators is complete. Suppose g is a function of unit norm in H^2 such that g^2 is rigid. Let the function b in the unit ball of H^∞ be defined as above, and let u be an inner function that divides the inner factor of b and vanishes at the origin. Is $T_g\mathcal{H}(u)$ then necessarily the kernel of a Toeplitz operator?

Hayashi showed in [S3] that the last question has a negative answer, and he described how to construct the most general proper subspace of H^2 that can serve as the kernel of a Toeplitz operator. Here is his recipe. One starts with a function f in H^2 such that f^2 is rigid, and an inner function u such that $u(0) = 0$. Let b_0 be the function in the unit ball of H^∞ such that the real part of $\dfrac{1+b_0}{1-b_0}$ is the Poisson integral of $|f|^2$, and such that $b_0(0)$ is real. Let $b = ub_0$, let the function a be defined as usual, and let $g = \dfrac{a}{1-b}$. (By (NX-5), the function g^2 is rigid.) Then $Tg\mathcal{H}(u)$ is the kernel of a Toeplitz operator (in fact, of $T_{\overline{ug}/g}$), and by this method one constructs the most general proper subspace of H^2 that is such a kernel.

A more detailed account of these matters, emphasizing the role of de Branges-Rovnyak spaces, can be found in [S11].

(XI-3) Multipliers. Information about the multipliers of $\mathcal{H}(b)$ is scattered above. One relatively simple result, given in (IV-6), is that, if b is nonextreme, then every function holomorphic on $\overline{D}$ is a multiplier of $\mathcal{H}(b)$. If b is extreme, on the other hand, it is more difficult to produce multipliers of $\mathcal{H}(b)$. In fact, it is not hard to show that if b is an inner function then

$\mathcal{H}(b)$ has no nonconstant multipliers.

In [44] B. A. Lotto and the author studied the multipliers of $\mathcal{H}(b)$ for the case where b is extreme but not an inner function. It was shown that $\mathcal{H}(b)$ has an abundance of multipliers in this case. For example, if b is extreme then every multiplier of $\mathcal{H}(b)$ differs by a constant from a function in $\mathcal{H}(\bar{b})$, and the ones that lie in $\mathcal{H}(\bar{b})$ are dense in $\mathcal{H}(\bar{b})$. F. D. Suárez continued the study in [S16], making significant progress.

Concerning the case where b is nonextreme, the paper [20] of B. M. Davis and J. E. McCarthy has already been noted. The only subsequent work seems to be the paper [S6] of Lotto and the author.

The problem of finding a reasonably concrete characterization of the multipliers of $\mathcal{H}(b)$ for the general case is perhaps unreasonably difficult. Nevertheless, further study of multipliers is bound to augment our understanding of the structure of $\mathcal{H}(b)$.

(XI-4) **Holomorphic Composition Operators.** The composition operator induced by the function b, denoted C_b, acts on any function defined in D according to the formula $(C_b f)(z) = f(b(z))$. These operators act boundedly on many Banach spaces of holomorphic functions in D, including the space H^2. An interesting problem has been to determine when the operator C_b acts compactly on H^2. The problem, along with its analogue in other spaces, was studied by J. H. Shapiro and P. D. Taylor in [S15], and thirteen years later by B. D. MacCluer and Shapiro in [S7]. One year after that, in a paper that has stimulated much of the current interest in holomorphic composition operators, Shapiro [S12] found a beautiful necessary and sufficient condition for the compactness of C_b on H^2. Shapiro's monograph [S13] gives an interesting account of these developments.

Shapiro and Taylor noted that if C_b acts compactly on H^2 then b cannot have an angular derivative in the sense of Carathéodory at any point of ∂D. MacCluer and Shapiro proved that the converse holds when b has finite valence. The converse does not hold in general, however. For example, it is easy to see that C_b does not give a compact operator on H^2 when b is an inner function, while O. Frostman [25] has constructed Blaschke products that lack angular derivatives in the sense of Carathéodory. The necessary and sufficient condition of Shapiro, which will not be stated precisely here, involves the Nevanlinna counting function for b. Roughly, it requires that b not assume values near ∂D "too often."

Another necessary and sufficient condition for C_b to act compactly on H^2, very different in appearance from Shapiro's, arose from the author's paper [S9]. The condition is that all of the measures μ_λ associated with b (as in Chapter III—see also (NX-6)) be absolutely continuous with respect to Lebesgue measure. The sufficiency of the condition was established in [S9] and the necessity by Shapiro and C. Sundberg in [S14]. (Sundberg subsequently found a simpler proof of the necessity; it has not yet been published.) A direct function-theoretic proof of the equivalence of the absolute continuity condition with Shapiro's counting function condition is still lacking.

The propositions (IV-8) and (V-9) on comparison of measures enable one to state the absolute continuity condition for the compactness of C_b on H^2 in a form that can be recognized as a strengthening of the necessary condition involving angular derivatives. As pointed out in (VI-8), the function b has an angular derivative in the sense of Carathéodory at the point z_0 in ∂D if and only if there is a point λ in ∂D such that the function $\dfrac{\operatorname{Re}(1 - \overline{\lambda}b)}{\operatorname{Re}(1 - \overline{z}_0 z)}$ is in L^1 of ∂D. Thus, for b to have no angular derivative in the sense of Carathéodory, it is necessary and sufficient that the function $\dfrac{\operatorname{Re}(1 - \overline{\lambda}b)}{\operatorname{Re}(1 - \overline{z}_0 z)}$ fail to be in L^1 for every λ in ∂D and every z_0 in ∂D. This statement comes from the special cases of (IV-8) and (V-9) in which the singular measures involved are point masses. Using the full strength of (IV-8) and (V-9), but otherwise arguing as before, one concludes that the measure μ_λ has a nonzero singular component if and only if there is a nonconstant inner function u such that the function $\dfrac{\operatorname{Re}(1 - \overline{\lambda}b)}{\operatorname{Re}(1 - u)}$ is in L^1. Thus: *the operator C_b acts compactly on H^2 if and only if the function $\dfrac{\operatorname{Re}(1 - \overline{\lambda}b)}{\operatorname{Re}(1 - u)}$ fails to be in L^1 for every point λ in ∂D and every nonconstant inner function u.*

REFERENCES

1. V. M. Adamyan, D. Z. Arov and M. G. Krein, *Infinite Hankel matrices and generalized problems of Carathéodory-Fejér and I. Schur*, Funkcional. Anal. i Prilozhen. **2** (1968), vyp. 4, 1–17.
2. P. R. Ahern and D. N. Clark, *Radial limits and invariant subspaces*, Amer. J. Math. **92** (1970), 332–342.
3. P. R. Ahern and D. N. Clark, *Radial N-th derivatives of Blaschke products*, Math. Scand. **28** (1971), 189–201.
4. D. Alpay and H. Dym, *Hilbert spaces of analytic functions, inverse scattering, and operator models* I, Integral Equations and Operator Theory **7** (1984), 589–641.
5. D. Alpay and H. Dym, *Hilbert spaces of analytic functions, inverse scattering, and operator models* II, Integral Equations and Operator Theory **8** (1985), 145–180.
6. N. Aronszajn, *Theory of reproducing kernels*, Trans. Amer. Math. Soc. **68** (1950), 337–404.
7. J. A. Ball, *Unitary perturbations of contractions*, Dissertation, University of Virginia (1973).
8. J. A. Ball and N. Cohen, *de Branges–Rovnyak operator models and systems theory: A survey*, Operator Theory: Advances and Applications, Vol. 50, Birkhäuser, Basel (1991), 93–136.
9. J. A. Ball and T. L. Kriete, *Operator-valued Nevanlinna–Pick kernels and the functional models for contractions*, Integral Equations and Operator Theory **10** (1987), 17–61.
10. J. A. Ball and A. Lubin, *On a class of contractive perturbations of restricted shifts*, Pacific J. Math. **63** (1976), 309–323.
11. P. Bloomfield, N. P. Jewell and E. Hayashi, *Characterizations of completely nondeterministic stochastic processes*, Pacific J. Math. **107** (1983), 307–317.

12. L. de Branges, *Underlying concepts in the proof of the Bieberbach conjecture*, Proceedings of the International Congress of Mathematicians (Berkeley, 1986), Berkeley, 1987, 25–42.
13. L. de Branges, *Square Summable Power Series*, forthcoming.
14. L. de Branges and J. Rovnyak, *Square Summable Power Series*, Holt, Rinehart and Winston, New York, 1966.
15. L. de Branges and J. Rovnyak, *Appendix on square summable power series*, in "Perturbation Theory and its Applications in Quantum Mechanics", John Wiley and Sons, New York (1966), 347–392.
16. C. Carathéodory, *Über die Winkelderivierten von beschränkten Funktionen*, Sitzungber. Preuss. Akad. Wiss. (1929), 39–52.
17. J. A. Cima and T. H. MacGregor, *Cauchy transforms of measures and univalent functions*, Lecture Notes in Math., Vol. 1275, Springer, Berlin (1978), 78–88.
18. D. N. Clark, *One dimensional perturbations of restricted shifts*, J. Analyse Math. **25** (1972), 169–191.
19. C. C. Cowen and Ch. Pommerenke, *Inequalities for the angular derivative of an analytic function in the unit disk*, J. London Math. Soc. (2) **26** (1982), 271–289.
20. B. M. Davis and J. E. McCarthy, *Multipliers of de Branges' spaces*, Michigan Math. J. **38** (1991), 225–240.
21. A. Denjoy, *Sur l'itération des fonctions analytiques*, Comptes Rendus Acad. Sci. Paris **182** (1926), 255–257.
22. R. G. Douglas, *On majorization, factorization, and range inclusion of operators on Hilbert space*, Proc. Amer. Math. Soc. **17** (1966), 413–415.
23. R. G. Douglas, H. S. Shapiro and A. L. Shields, *Cyclic vectors and invariant subspaces for the backward shift operator*, Ann. Inst. Fourier **20** (1970), 37–76.
24. H. Dym, *J Contractive Matrix Functions, Reproducing Kernel Hilbert Spaces and Interpolation*, CBMS Regional Conference Series in Math., No. 71, Amer. Math. Soc., Providence, 1989.
25. O. Frostman, *Sur les produits de Blaschke*, Fysiogr. Sällsk. Lund Förh., **12** (1942), 169–182.
26. J. García-Cuerva and J. L. Rubio de Francia, *Weighted Norm Inequalities and Related Topics*, North-Holland, Amsterdam, 1985.
27. J. B. Garnett, *Bounded Analytic Functions*, Academic Press, New York,

1981.
28. P. R. Halmos, *Normal dilations and extensions of operators*, Summa Brasil. Math. **2** (1950), 125–134.
29. V. P. Havin, *On analytic functions representable by an integral of Cauchy-Stieltjes type*, Vestnik Leningrad. Univ. Ser. Math. Meh. Astr. **13** (1958), 66–79.
30. E. Hayashi, *The solution sets of extremal problems in H^1*, Proc. Amer. Math. Soc. **93** (1985), 690–696.
31. E. Hayashi, *The kernel of a Toeplitz operator*, Integral Equations and Operator Theory **9** (1986), 588–591.
32. H. Helson, *Large analytic functions*, Operator Theory: Advances and Applications, Vol. 43, Birkhäuser, Basel (1990), 209–216.
33. H. Helson, *Large analytic functions II*, Analysis and Partial Differential Equations, C. Sadosky (ed.), Marcel Dekker, New York (1990), 217–220.
34. H. Helson and D. Sarason, *Past and future*, Math. Scand. **21** (1967), 5–16.
35. K. Hoffman, *Banach Spaces of Analytic Functions*, Prentice-Hall, Englewood Cliffs, N.J., 1962.
36. J. Inoue and T. Nakazi, *Polynomials of an inner function which are exposed in H^1*, Proc. Amer. Math. Soc. **100** (1987), 454–456.
37. K. Izuchi and R. Younis, *On the unit ball of H^1 and boundary points*, preprint.
38. G. Julia, *Mémoire sur l'itération des fonctions rationnelles*, J. de Math. Pures et Appliq. (8) **1** (1918), 47–245.
39. G. Julia, *Extension nouvelle d'un lemme de Schwarz*, Acta Math. **42** (1920), 349–355.
40. E. Landau and G. Valiron, *A deduction from Schwarz's lemma*, J. London Math. Soc. **4** (1929), 162–163.
41. K. de Leeuw and W. Rudin, *Extreme points and extremum problems in H_1*, Pacific J. Math. **8** (1958), 467–485.
42. K. Y. Li, *Inequalities for fixed points of holomorphic functions*, Bull. London Math. Soc. **22** (1990), 446–452.
43. B. A. Lotto, *Inner multipliers of de Branges's spaces*, Integral Equations and Operator Theory **13** (1990), 216–230.
44. B. A. Lotto and D. Sarason, *Multiplicative structure of de Branges's spaces*, Rev. Mat. Iberoamericana **7** (1991), 183–220.

45. T. Nakazi, *Exposed points and extremal problems in H^1*, J. Functional Analysis **53** (1983), 224–230.
46. T. Nakazi, *Exposed points and extremal problems in H^1, II*, Tôhoku Math. J. **37** (1985), 265–269.
47. T. Nakazi, *Kernels of Toeplitz operators*, J. Math. Soc. Japan **38** (1986), 607–616.
48. J. Neuwirth and D. J. Newman, *Positive $H^{1/2}$ functions are constants*, Proc. Amer. Math. Soc. **18** (1987), 958.
49. R. Nevanlinna, *Remarques sur le lemme de Schwarz*, Comptes Rendu Acad. Sci. Paris **188** (1929), 1027–1029.
50. R. Nevanlinna, *Über beschränkte analytische Funktionen*, Ann. Acad. Sci. Fenn. Ser. A **32** (1929), No. 7.
51. N. K. Nikolskii and V. I. Vasyunin, *Notes on two function models*, in "The Bieberbach Conjecture – Proceedings of the Symposium on the Occasion of the Proof", Amer. Math. Soc., Providence (1986), 113–141.
52. N. K. Nikolskii and V. I. Vasyunin, *A unified approach to function models and the transcription problem*, Operator Theory: Advances and Applications, Vol. 41, Birkhäuser, Basel (1988), 405–434.
53. N. K. Nikolskii and V. I. Vasyunin, *Quasiorthogonal decompositions with respect to supplementary metrics and estimates of univalent functions*, Algebra i Analiz **4** (1990), vyp. 4, 1–81.
54. M. Riesz, *Sur certaines inégalités dans la théorie des fonctions*, Fysiogr. Sällsk. Lund Förh., **1** (1931), Nr. 4, 18–38.
55. W. Rudin, *Real and Complex Analysis*, McGraw-Hill, New York, Third Edition, 1987.
56. D. Sarason, *The H^p spaces of an annulus*, Memoirs Amer. Math. Soc., No. 56 (1965).
57. D. Sarason, *Function Theory on the Unit Circle*, Virginia Polytechnic Institute and State University, Blacksburg, Virginia, 1979.
58. D. Sarason, *Shift-invariant spaces from the Brangesian point of view*, in "The Bieberbach Conjecture – Proceedings of the Symposium on the Occasion of the Proof", Amer. Math. Soc., Providence (1986), 153–166.
59. D. Sarason, *Doubly shift-invariant spaces in H^2*, J. Operator Theory **16** (1986), 75–97.
60. D. Sarason, *Nearly invariant subspaces of the backward shift*, Operator Theory: Advances and Applications, Vol. 35, Birkhäuser, Basel (1988),

481–493.
61. D. Sarason, *Angular derivatives via Hilbert space*, Complex Variables **10** (1988), 1–10.
62. D. Sarason, *Exposed points in H^1*, I, Operator Theory: Advances and Applications, Vol. 41, Birkhäuser, Basel (1989), 485–496.
63. D. Sarason, *Exposed points in H^1*, II, Operator Theory: Advances and Applications, Vol. 48, Birkhäuser, Basel (1990), 333–347.
64. A. L. Shields and L. J. Wallen, *The commutants of certain Hilbert space operators*, Indiana Univ. Math. J. **20** (1971), 777–788.
65. B. Sz.-Nagy and C. Foias, *Harmonic Analysis of Operators on Hilbert Space*, North-Holland, Amsterdam, 1970.
66. B. Sz.-Nagy and C. Foias, *On contractions similar to isometries and Toeplitz operators*, Ann. Acad. Sci. Fennicae, Ser. A. I. Math. **2** (1976), 553–564.
67. S. A. Vinogradov, *Properties of multipliers of Cauchy–Stieltjes type integrals and some factorization problems for analytic functions*, in "Theory of Functions and Functional Analysis", Central Ekonom.-Mat. Inst. Akad. Nauk SSSR, Moscow (1976), 5–39: Amer. Math. Soc. Transl. (2), Vol. 115 (1980), 1–32.
68. J. Wolff, *Sur l'itération des fonctions holomorphes dans une région, et dont les valeurs appartiennent a cette région*, Comptes Rendus Acad. Sci. Paris **182** (1926), 42–43.
69. J. Wolff, *Sur l'itération des fonctiones bournées*, Comptes Rendus Acad. Sci. Paris **182** (1926), 200–201.
70. J. Wolff, *Sur une généralisation d'un théorém de Schwarz*, Comptes Rendus Acad. Sci. Paris **182** (1926), 918–920.
71. K. Yabuta, *Remarks on extremum problems in H^1*, Tôhoku Math. J. **23** (1971), 129–137.
72. K. Yabuta, *Some uniqueness theorems for $H^p(U^n)$ functions*, Tôhoku Math. J. **24** (1972), 353–357.
73. R. Younis, *Subordination and H^p functions*, Proc. Amer. Math. Soc. **110** (1990), 653–660.

SUPPLEMENTARY REFERENCES

S 1. R. G. Douglas, *Banach Algebra Techniques in Operator Theory*, Academic Press, New York and London, 1972.

S 2. P. L. Duren, *Theory of H^p Spaces*, Academic Press, New York and London, 1970.

S 3. E. Hayashi, *On the classification of nearly invariant subspaces of the backward shift*, Proc. Amer. Math. Soc. **110** (1990), 441–448.

S 4. D. Hitt, *Invariant subspaces of H^2 of an annulus*, Pacific J. Math. **134** (1988), 101–120.

S 5. J. Inoue *An example of a non-exposed extremal function in the unit ball of H^1*, Proc. Edinburgh Math. Soc. **37** (1993), 47–51.

S 6. B. A. Lotto and D. Sarason, *Multipliers of de Branges-Rovnyak spaces*, Indiana Univ. Math. J. **42** (1993), 907–920.

S 7. B. D. MacCluer and J. H. Shapiro, *Angular derivatives and compact composition operators on the Hardy and Bergman spaces*, Canadian J. Math. **38** (1986), 878–906.

S 8. A. G. Poltoratskii, *Boundary behavior of pseudocontinuable functions*, Algebra i Analiz **5** (1993), 189–210.

S 9. D. Sarason, *Composition operators as integral operators*, Analysis and Partial Differential Equations, C. Sadosky (ed.), Marcel-Dekker, New York, (1990), 545–565.

S10. D. Sarason, *Making an outer function from two inner functions*, Contemporary Mathematics **137** (1992), Amer. Math. Soc., Providence, 407–414.

S11. D. Sarason, *Kernels of Toeplitz operators*, Operator Theory: Advances and Applications (to appear).

S12. J. H. Shapiro, *The essential norm of a composition operator*, Annals of Math. **125** (1987), 375–404.

S13. J. H. Shapiro, *Composition Operators and Classical Function Theory*, Springer-Verlag, New York, 1993.

S14. J. H. Shapiro and C. Sundberg, *Compact composition operators on L^1*, Proc. Amer. Math. Soc. **108** (1990), 443–449.

S15. J. H. Shapiro and P. D. Taylor, *Compact, nuclear, and Hilbert-Schmidt composition operators on H^2*, Indiana Univ. Math. J. **125** (1973), 471–496.

S16. F. D. Suárez, *Multipliers of de Branges-Rovnyak spaces in H^2*, Rev. Mat. Iberoamericana (to appear).

S17. F. D. Suárez, *Backward shift invariant spaces in H^2*, preprint.

S18. D. Zheng, *Products of Toeplitz operators and Hankel operators*, preprint.

INDEX

Adamyan, V. M., 81, 85
Ahern, P. R., 56, 85
Alpay, D., 14, 22, 85
Angular derivative, 46ff.
Angular derivative in the sense of Carathéodory, 48, 83
Aronszajn, N., 7, 85
Arov, D. Z., 81, 85
Backward shift, v
Ball, J. A., 14, 22, 35, 85
Bieberbach conjecture, 7
Bloomfield, P., 79, 80, 85
Bounded containment, 1
de Branges, L., i, 7, 14, 56, 64, 86
de Branges-Rovnyak model theory, i, 35
de Branges–Rovnyak space, i, 10
Carathéodory, C., 46, 56, 86
Carathéodory's theorem on angular derivatives, 48, 56
Carleson, L., 62
Cauchy integral, 15ff.
Characteristic operator function, 64
Cima, J. A., 22, 86
Clark, D. N., 22, 56, 85, 86
Cohen, N., 14, 85

Complementary space, i, 3, 7
Composition operator, 83
Contractive containment, 1
Corona pair, 62, 66
Corona theorem, 62, 64
Cowen, C. C., 56, 86
Cyclic vector (of the backward shift), 38, 45
Davis, B. M., 14, 22, 35, 69, 83, 86
Denjoy, A., 46, 56, 86
Denjoy–Wolff point, 53, 56
Denjoy–Wolff theorem, 54, 56
Devinatz, A., 66
Devinatz–Widom theorem, 66
Disk algebra, 19
Douglas, R. G., iii, 2, 45, 86, 90
Douglas's criterion, 2, 7, 63, 67
Duren, P. L., iii, 90
Dym, H., 14, 22, 56, 85, 86
Exposed point, 35, 72, 79
Extreme point, 22, 35, 37ff., 79
Fixed point, 53
Foias, C., 35, 45, 64, 89
Frostman, O., 56, 83, 86

93

Garcia-Cuervo, J., 69, 86
Garnett, J. B., iii, 64, 69, 81, 86
Gaussian sequence, completely nondeterministic, 79
Halmos, P. R., 7, 87
Havin, V. P., 22, 87
Hayashi, E., 79, 80, 82, 85, 87, 90
Helson, H., 65, 79, 80, 87
Helson–Szegő theorem, 65, 68, 69
Helson–Szegő weight, 65, 68, 78
Herglotz integral, 17
Hitt, D., 22, 81, 90
Hitt's theorem, 81
Hoffman, K., 35, 45, 87
Hunt, R., 65
Hunt–Muckenhoupt–Wheeden theorem, 65, 69
Identity for difference quotients, 61, 64
Inoue, J., 79, 80, 87, 90
Integral of Cauchy-Stieltjes type, 22
Invariant subspace, 35, 45
Izuchi, K., 79, 87
Jewell, N. P., 79, 80, 85
Julia, G., 56, 87
Julia, lemma of, 51, 56
Kapustin, V., 80
Kernel function, 9, 10
Kernel function for derivative, 58
Krein, M. G., 81, 85
Kriete, T. L., 14, 35, 85
Landau, E., 56, 87

de Leeuw, K., 79, 87
Li, K. Y., 56, 87
Lindelöf, E., 64
Lindelöf's theorem, 64
Linear manifold, v
Lotto, B. A., 7, 14, 22, 64, 83, 87, 90
Lubin, A., 14, 22, 85
MacCluer, B. D., 83, 90
MacGregor, T. H., 22, 86
McCarthy, J. E., 14, 22, 35, 69, 83, 86
Muckenhoupt, B., 65
Muckenhoupt's condition (A_2), 65
Multiplication operator, 12
Multiplier, 12, 19, 22, 26, 60, 67, 82
Nakazi, T., 79, 80, 87, 88
Nearly invariant subspace of the backward shift, 81
Nehari interpolation problem, 81
Neuwirth, J., 79, 88
Nevanlinna, R., 56, 88
Newman, D. J., 79, 88
Nikolskii, N. K., 7, 14, 88
Noncyclic vector (of the backward shift), 38, 45
Nonextreme point, 22ff.
Operator range, 1
Overlapping space, 3, 4, 8, 10
Poltoratskii, A. G., 22, 90
Pommerenke, Ch., 56, 86
Prediction theory, 79, 80
Quasiaffinity, 72
Quasisimilarity, 72
Riesz, M., 56, 88

Riesz, theorem of F.
   and M., 21, 30
Rigid function, 70ff., 79, 81
Rovnyak, J., i, 7, 14, 64, 86
Rubio de Francia, J. L., 69, 86
Rudin, W., 79, 87, 88
Sarason, D., 7, 14, 22, 35, 56
   64, 79, 80, 81, 83, 84, 87,
   88, 89, 90
Shapiro, H. S., 45, 86
Shapiro, J. H., 46, 83, 90, 91
Shields, A. L., 14, 45, 86, 89
Shift operator, v
Smirnov class, 35
Suárez, F. D., 45, 83, 91
Subspace, v
Sundberg, C., 84, 91
Szegö, G., 65
Sz.–Nagy, B., 35, 45, 64, 89
Sz.–Nagy–Foias model, i, 26, 35,
   40, 64
Taylor, P. D., 83, 91
Toeplitz operator, 9, 19, 30,
   66, 70, 81
Valiron, G., 56, 87
Vasyunin, V. I., 7, 14, 88
Vector subspace, v
Vinogradov, S. A., 22, 89
Wallen, L. J., 14, 89
Wheeden, R., 65
Widom, H., 66
Wolff, J., 46, 56, 89
Yabuta, K., 79, 89
Younis, R., 79, 87, 89
Zheng, D., 35, 91